CW01261227

Glover Family

English Combat Fighting System

TRAINING BOOK

English Combat

By
Terry Glover B.E.M.

First Edition
2004

My thanks go to Sam Martin, Adam Speake, Ashley Brown, Tonya Glover and AJ for modelling and demonstrating the techniques for the photographs in this training book. Also, my congratulations go to Sam Martin on his selection for the British Stickfighting Team to compete at the World full-contact Stickfighting Championships in Cebu, Philippines in June 2004.

Copyright © 2004 Terry Glover B.E.M.
All rights reserved. No part of this publication may be reproduced, stored in a retrieval system, or transmitted, in any form or by any means, electronic, mechanical, photocopying, recording, or otherwise, without the written prior permission of the author or publisher.

Written and illustrated by Terry Glover B.E.M.

First Edition

ISBN 0-9547404-3-2

Typeset and produced by Terry Glover B.E.M. and Ashley Brown

Graphic design and photography by Ashley Brown

Published by Quarterstaff Publishing, Nottingham, England.   EC002
www.englishcombat.com

Printed in Hong Kong by Regal Printing, 2004.

*This book is dedicated with love to Tonya, Edward and Li.
They are the reason I have achieved so much in my life.*

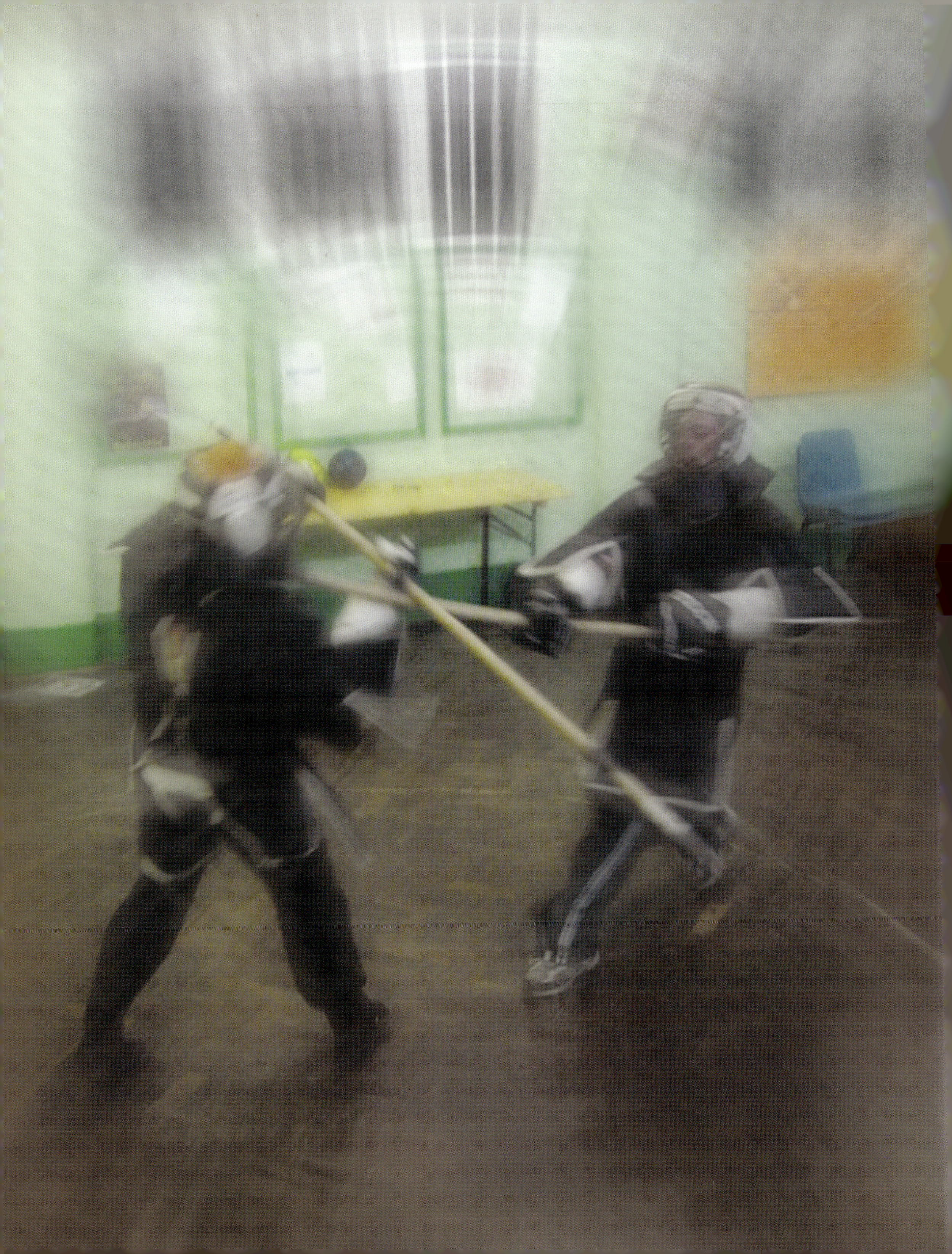

CONTENTS

English Combat 7
Foreword 9
Introduction 11
    Equipment 11
    List to complete before commencement 12
    Words of command 12
    Stances 13
    Weapon grips 13
    English Broadsword Circle 14
    Skipping 15
    Basic 'on guard' 16
    Blocking 17

Chapter I: The Basics 19
    Movement 19
    Blocks 19
    Kicking 23
    Focus 24
   Armed 25
    Quarterstaff 25
    Short Staff or Cudgel 29
    Knife 31
   Combinations 33
    Unarmed 33
    Armed 33
    Combination One 34
    Combination Two 37

Chapter II: Takedowns 39
    Unarmed 39
    Armed 47
    The Long-range drill 48
    The Medium-range drill 49
    The Short-range drill 52
    Knife Stripping 54
    Combinations 56

Chapter III: Releases 59
    Attacking for Defence 69
    Focus 70

Chapter IV: Weapons Skills – Including Disarms 73
    The Whip 73
    Knife Throwing 76
    Throwing the Axe 78
    The Quarterstaff Throw 78
    Quarterstaff Disarms 79
    Stick Disarms 81

Chapter V: Advanced Weapon skills 93
- The Bull Whip 93
- The Ball and Chain 96
- Knife 98
- The Axe 102
- The Quarter Staff 105

Chapter VI: Special Skills 107
- Doorway Practice 107
- Stairway Practice 107
- Dealing With Gang Attacks 108
- Techniques that are helpful to a Lady 109
- Dealing with Bullies at School 114
- Dealing with Bullies at Work 115
- Daily objects as weapons 115

Chapter VII: The Syllabus 123
Instructor Assessment 123
Syllabus - Part One 124
- Basics 124
- Combinations 124
Syllabus - Part Two 125
- Basics 125
- Combinations 125
Syllabus - Part Three 126
- Basics 126
- Combinations 126
Syllabus - Part Four 127
- Weapon Demonstration 127
- Disarms 127
- Free Fighting 127

Competition Criteria 128
Full Contact Weapon Fighting: The Rules 129
The Competition Area 130

English Combat

The English Fighting System for self-defence and competition

English Combat teaches use of the English Quarterstaff, Single Stick, Double Stick, Knife, Axe, Whip, Ball and Chain and unarmed combat.

This system brings together English fighting techniques from all ages that made the Englishman the World's most feared and respected fighter.

This Training Book shows how to use these skills individually and in combination. The Syllabus is explained in writing and picture format with added line illustrations for ease of reference.

Read on and enjoy the experience of training and learning this simple proven English system.

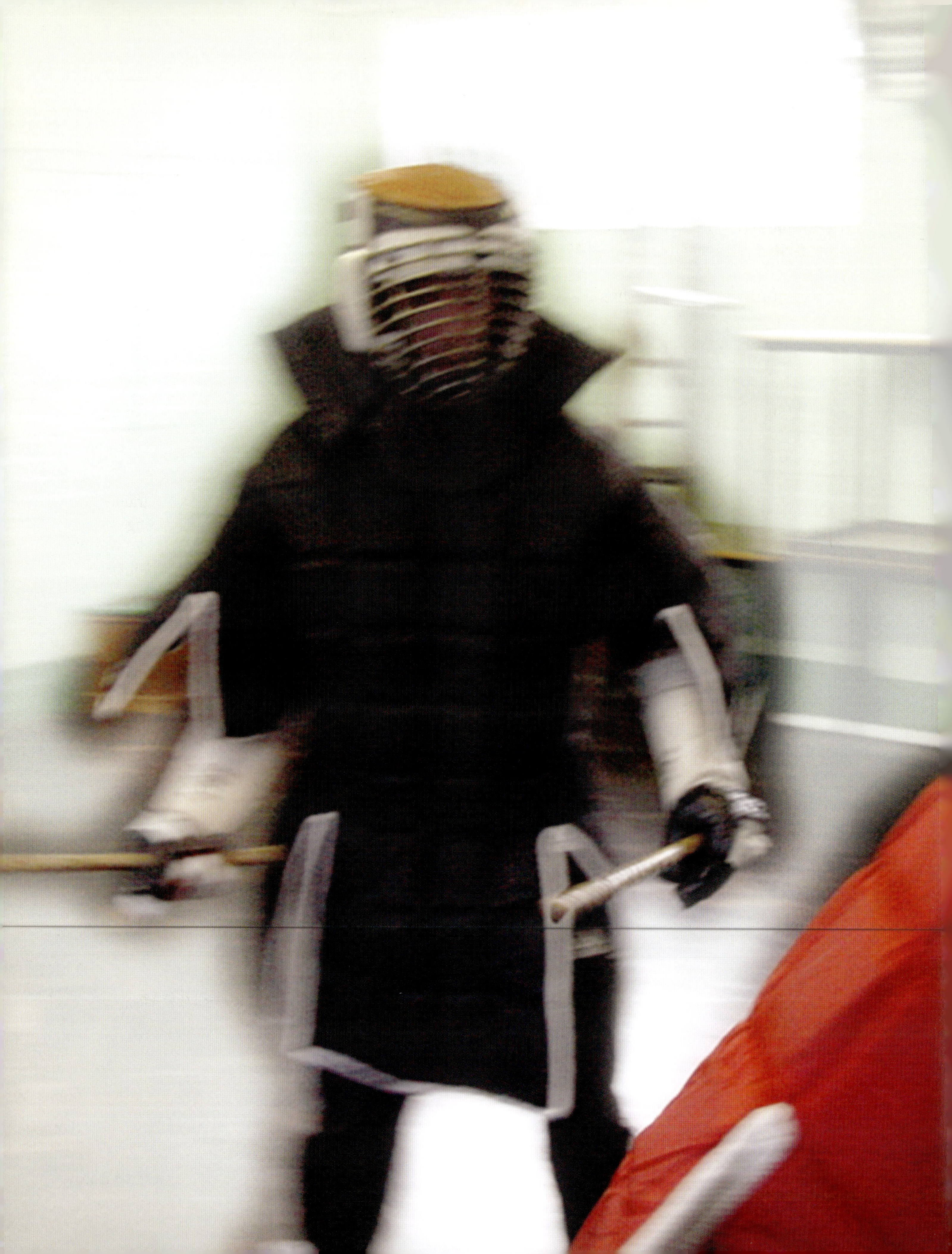

FOREWORD

The author is Mr T J P Glover B.E.M., Founder and Chief Instructor of the English Combat Fighting System. He is twice full-contact stick fighting World Champion (2000, 2001), five times British and four times English Champion.

"My love of fighting, in any shape or form, as a young boy was the main reason for following a path that would lead to the introduction of the Glover Family Fighting System to the World.

Whether it was punching, kicking, wrestling, hand held weapons (those designed to be used for close combat or thrown at an adversary), I loved them all. I was and still am fascinated by the human body and its myriad abilities.

Terry receiving the World Championship Trophy from Grand Master Cacoy Canete, Los Angeles, USA, 2001.

In my mind I was always uneasy as each style or art I trained in seemed somehow special at first, until time spent training showed me they were just the same techniques that my Grandfather had showed me when I was a child. They just had different names and were carried out in different ways.

I finished a journey along a path of fighting systems and decided to return to my native England, train fully in my family system and attempt to take the World by storm.

Having actually done this and stood upon the World stage acknowledged by my contemporary peers as World Champion, not just once but twice in two different World Associations, has justified my family fighting system. Read on and discover that you too can use English Combat to do the same."

This book is intended to elaborate upon the Glover Family English Combat Fighting System Syllabus, which is incorporated within the following descriptive chapters. On completing the content as detailed in this book, fighters will have gained new skills and added another string to their combat bow.

Each chapter will explain how to carry out the techniques used to complete each stage in the syllabus. Train hard and diligently.

Strive to be a Paladin

The DVD showing the system in visual format will follow in due course and will be a suitable addition for people intent on mastering this unique system.

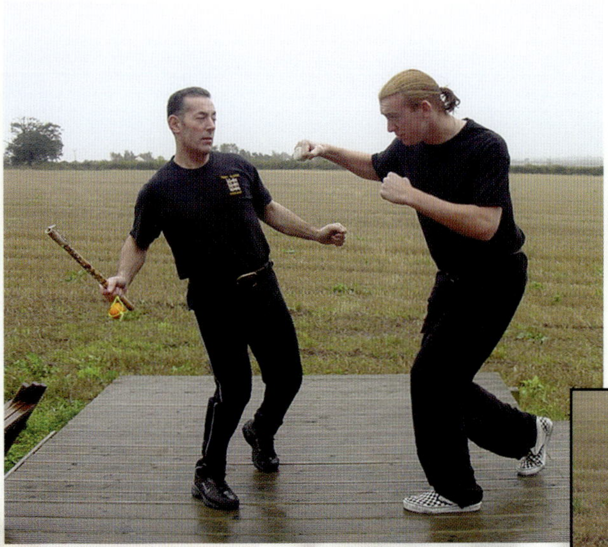
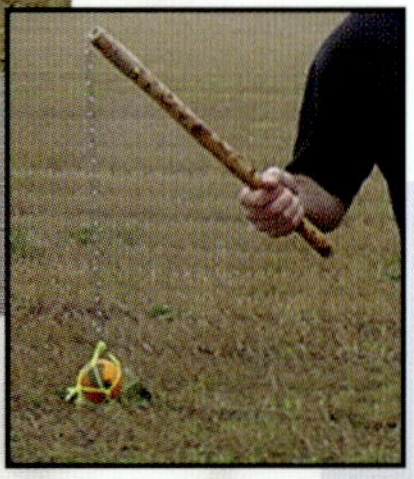
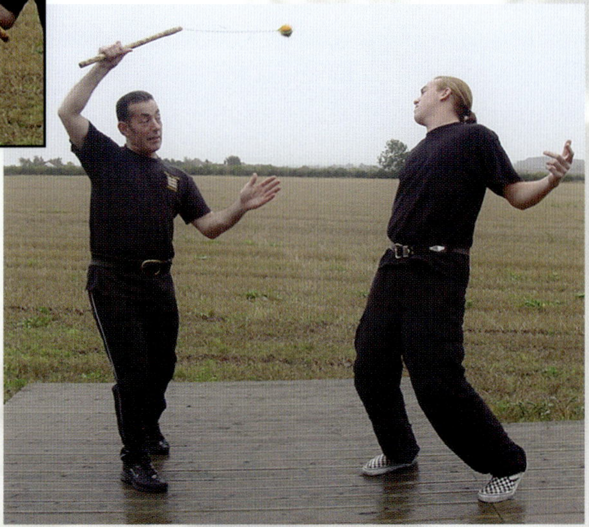
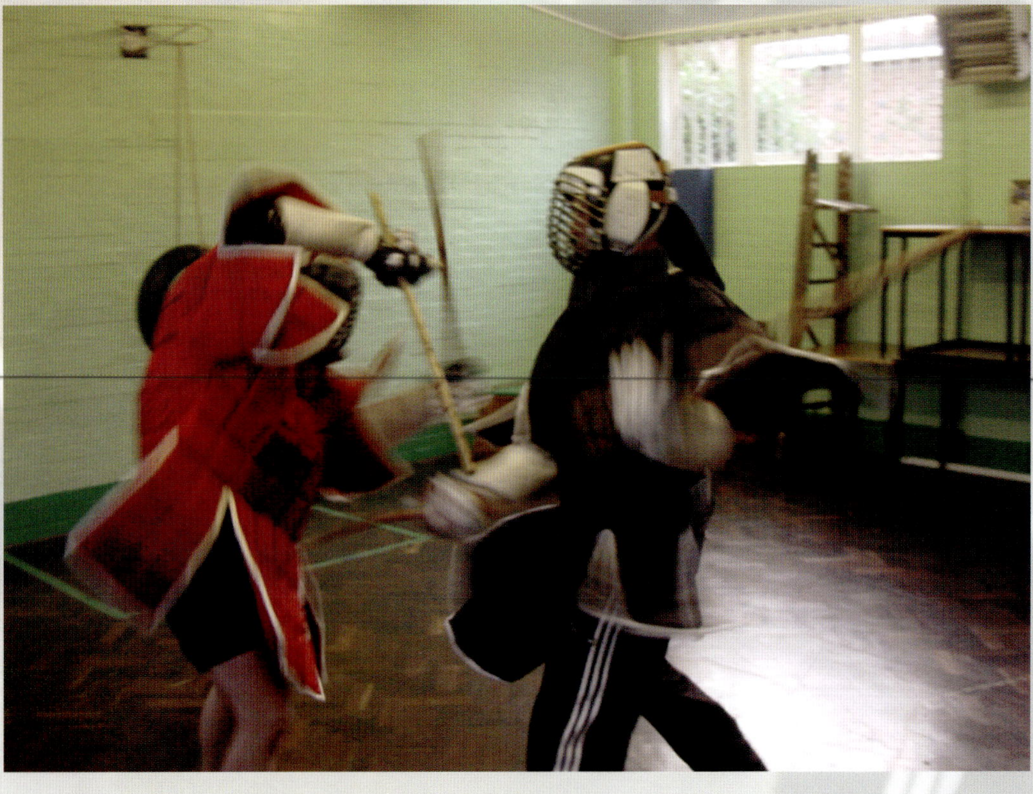

INTRODUCTION

No human being is invulnerable, so we that fight and train to fight must keep our bodies in a condition that will allow us to do so. The fighter must first have a medical check and then do the daily training outlined on the English Combat website training page. Once fit you can commence.

If you are offered the chance of training in a fighting system and the instructor says it will get you fit, walk away, you have just met a fool. Get fit to train in the system, not the other way around. Having achieved fitness, then continue.

**We have one life and one body.
Live long, stay healthy and enjoy them.**

Equipment

The equipment required for training in the English Combat system and taking part in competition is listed below:

- T-Shirt
- Training bottoms
- Training shoes
- Belt to hold up bottoms and carry weapons
- Two sticks made of rattan cane for safety when partner training, that are 3ft in length
- One Quarter Staff made of rattan, to be approximately the height plus one hand span of the fighter
- One wooden and one metal dagger, both blunted for safety
- One skipping rope of choice, although leather is best
- One suit of body armour, arm, hand and groin protection
- One roll of duct tape for ongoing repairs
- One ten-foot Bullwhip. Six-foot will do if ten-foot is scarce
- One single and one double ball and chain, rattan and rubber ball for training
- Various pads and wooden targets, hanging bags and tyres to practice targeting and focused impacting
- Spirit
- Determination
- Desire to be the victor

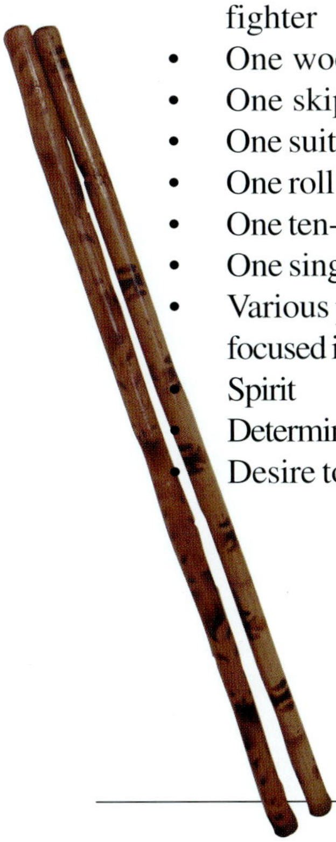

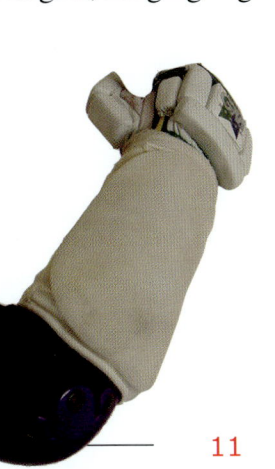

List to complete before commencement

To complete the system syllabus it is necessary to learn and practice the following:

- Words of command
- Stances
- Weapon grips
- The English Broadsword circle
- Skipping
- The basic on-guard
- Blocking

Words of command

In order to train with a group of fighters there is a need for safety. To facilitate this you must have only one person in charge of a group. This person will be the Instructor or leader and will need to issue all commands to run the session.

The words of command used in English Combat are as follows:

Prepare to move
This will warn all fighters that a command will be given.

Move
This will indicate that all fighters must carry out the command.

Stop
This is to be called to stop all movement. If the Instructor notices an unsafe practice, then fighters must freeze motion until informed what to do next. This will keep the session safe.

Fight
This is to indicate that sparring will begin. Unsupervised sparring is dangerous and unproductive. Once experience and ability is gained from long periods of training it is still good to have someone watch and comment on your skills in a constructive way.

Line up
This is so that the Instructor can see who is training and establish the beginning and end of the session.

On guard
This is used to bring fighters on their guard to commence an aspect of training. Once on guard, fighters must wait for the order to commence.

Stances

In English Combat there are no appreciable stances, it is set up so that you must respond to an attack if you are sitting, kneeling standing or even lying down. Each human being is built and moves differently to another. For me to say you must deliver a technique in a certain way would be foolish. It may work well for me but be unusable for you. You must fight often and well to learn how you adapt best in combat.

Some movements are common to all human shapes. These are used extensively.

If you accept that the majority of people are right-handed then it makes sense to always adopt a guard with your right side forward. This will give you an advantage on beginning the combat. You still need, however, to practice on both sides of the body so that you can accommodate an attacker from whatever attack angle is used against you.

Weapon grips

It is necessary to have the same grip on all weapons if it can be done. You may adjust for balance of a weapon but if you are unarmed, or armed, then the grip and guard should be the same.

Here is an illustration of this:

English Broadsword Circle

This is the basic set of angles used within English Combat. This was used centuries ago to enable instruction to be given to protagonists of the English Broadsword and Cudgel. These angles must be committed to memory before commencement. All techniques are carried out using these angles, whether they are for attack or defence.

The Circle is illustrated below:

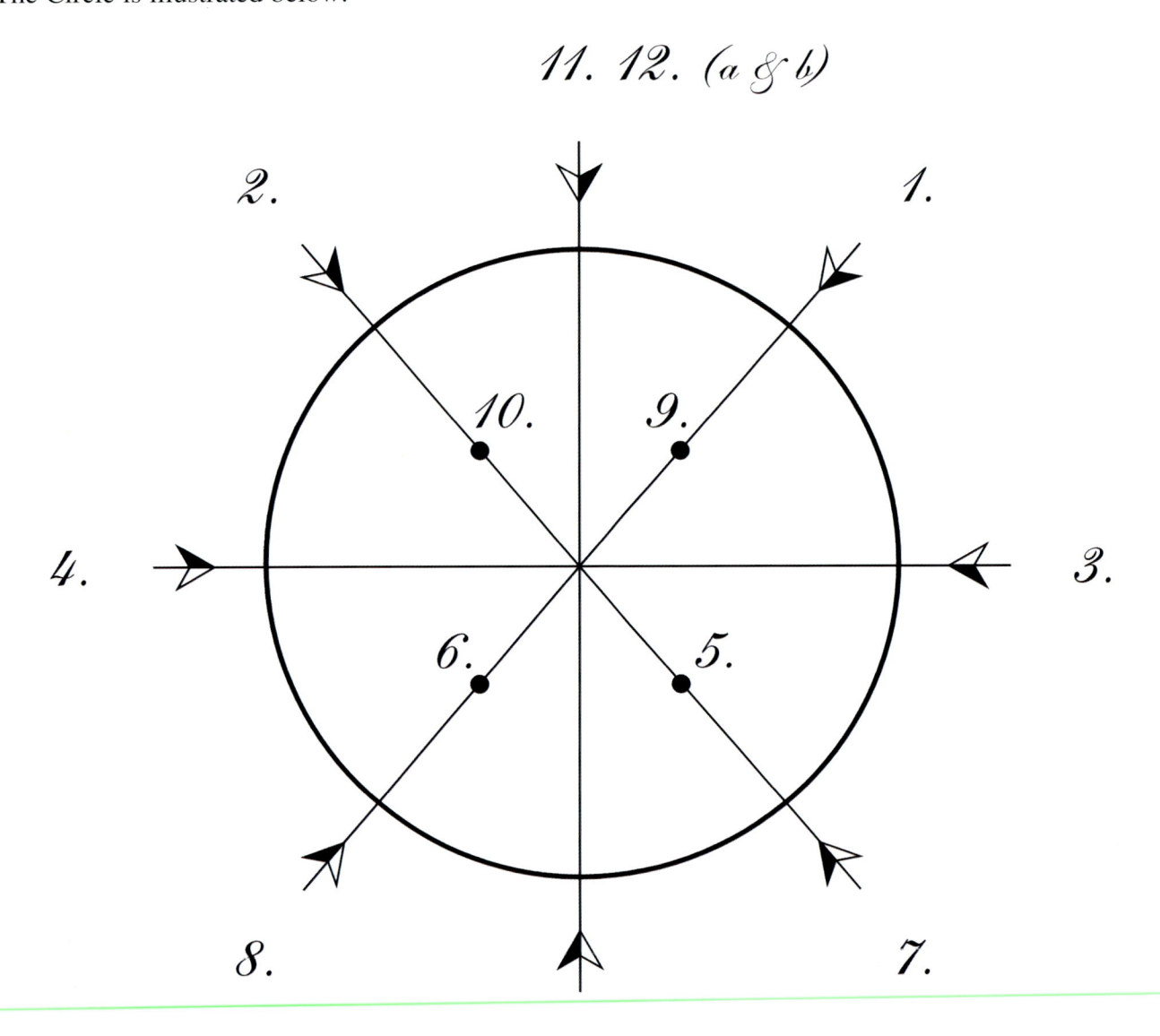

11. 12. (a & b)

2.   *1.*

10.   *9.*

4.   *3.*

6.   *5.*

8.   *7.*

As you face the diagram you must imagine you are holding a Stick in your right hand, standing in fighting stance and then pretend to slice the stick from the outside to the inside by following the arrow. Start with number one and continue. Do this with all the angles in practice.

Once the strike is started, flow through and allow the stick to flow back, instead of being taken back directly, to the fighting stance again.

Note that numbers 5, 6, 9 and 10 are thrusts and not sliced and therefore executed with the point of the stick.

The below illustration shows that the Stick or Cudgel is held one handgrip up from the base or butt.

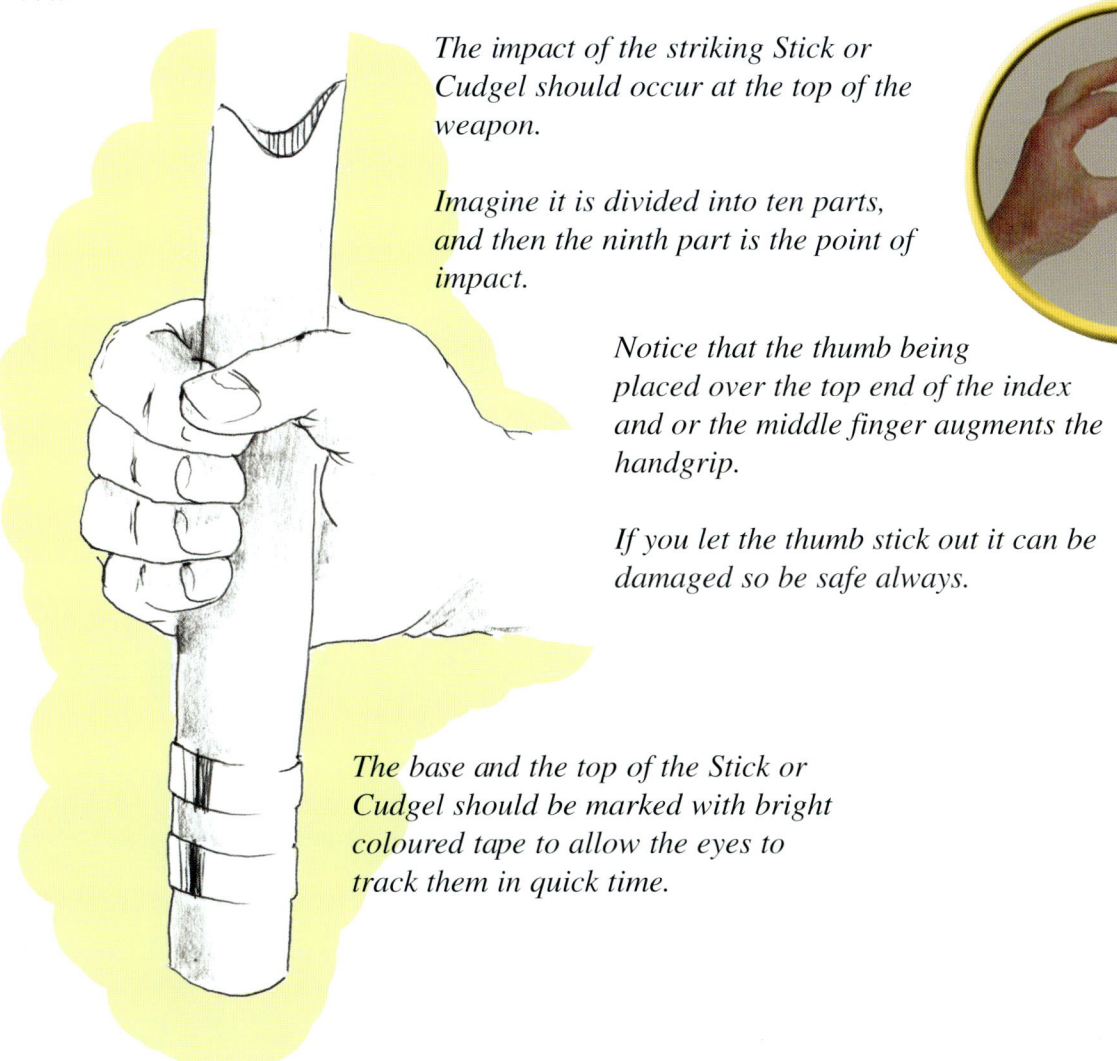

The impact of the striking Stick or Cudgel should occur at the top of the weapon.

Imagine it is divided into ten parts, and then the ninth part is the point of impact.

Notice that the thumb being placed over the top end of the index and or the middle finger augments the handgrip.

If you let the thumb stick out it can be damaged so be safe always.

The base and the top of the Stick or Cudgel should be marked with bright coloured tape to allow the eyes to track them in quick time.

Skipping

Skipping is badly underrated by some fighters. It is excellent for increasing hand and foot speed. The skips recommended here are by no means exhaustive and fighters will all no doubt have their own particular favourite. It is especially good for training at home if the weather is inclement as this may preclude a running session in some countries.

I would recommend starting with a double skip, which is passing the rope under the feet once to two jumps with both feet simultaneously and repeat. Follow this with single skips, which allow the rope to pass once, whilst you step with both feet simultaneously.

Once you are proficient at this then add boxer's skip, and now and again pass the rope under your feet twice before your feet touch the ground, while continuing skipping.

The difficult one to master and gain great aerobic benefits from is **Double-Dutch** skipping. This is not a problem to accomplish as most children can do it. If you spot a child doing it then ask them to show you how. They will be only too pleased.

To carry this type of skipping out you need to have two training partners, one on each end of rope holding onto two ropes each by the ends. You then have to be able to skip while both ropes are passed under your feet in quick succession. In America there are skipping competitions that accommodate this and if you have the chance then go along and watch or take part. It is excellent training.

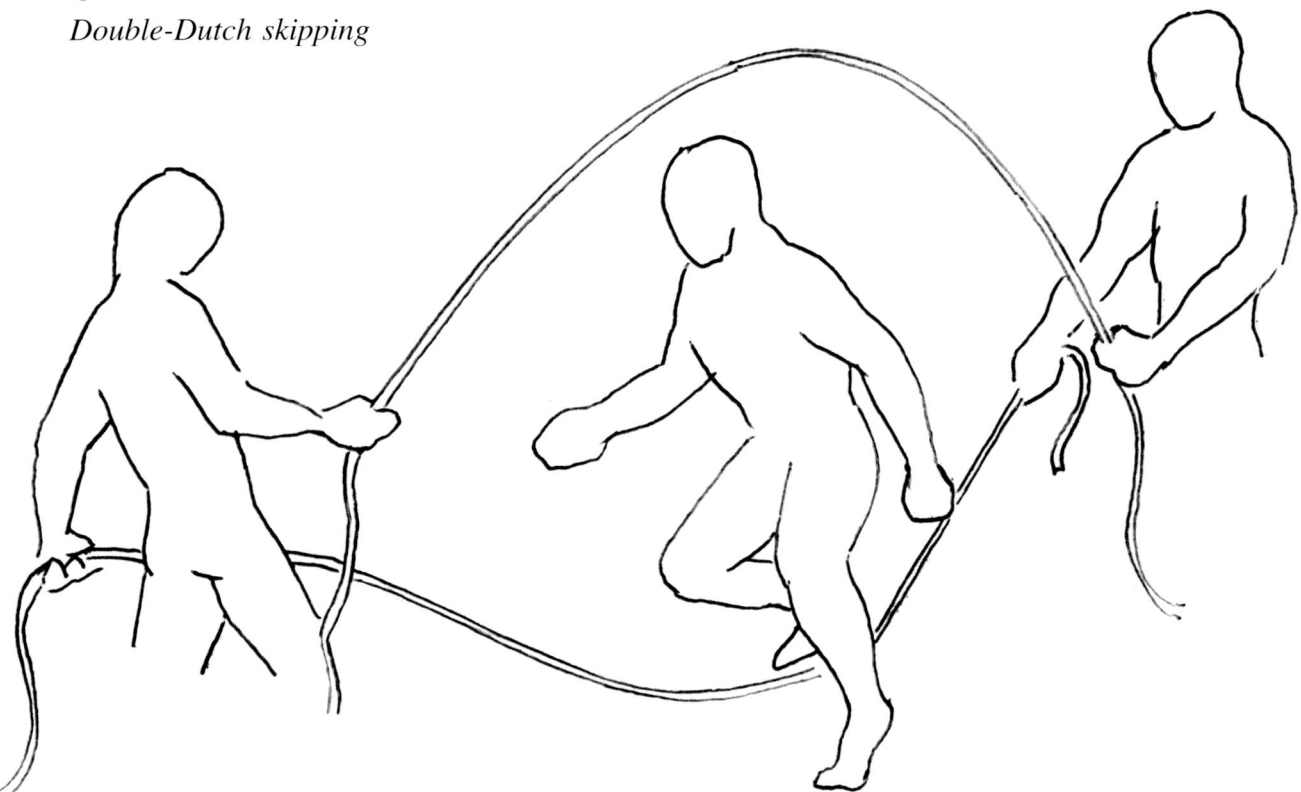

Double-Dutch skipping

Basic 'on guard'

Standing with one foot forward with the forward leg knee bent carries out the basic on guard (attackers break straight legs). The fighter must alter this stance constantly so that a fluid movement is adopted with which to throw appropriate techniques from a variety of angles.

The hands are held with the leading fist in line with the mouth and the rear hand in front of the belly button. Always remember, that as soon as combat commences your guard will constantly change. This is basic good sense on a battlefield. You start from a prepared position then once battle commences, become fluid on attack and defence, as this is a standard military maxim.

The advanced guard is not recommended until several years training has taken place and the fighter has acquired an arsenal of techniques. The advanced guard has the front arm low and the back fist high.

Blocking

Blocking is carried out in many ways and most are described in the following chapters. If you block a technique in a way unique to you and it works consistently, then "bravo". If it works, then remember it and continue to train it.

All seasoned fighters will know that in combat situations there are times when blocking is done by accident and in peculiar ways. This does not make them wrong, all systems, (this one is no different) require beginners to learn basic blocking to show how it can be done. Then you learn by experience, trial and error, which block is necessarily applied in any given situation.

The following chapters will lead the fighter through the requirements that will enable you to know and practice English Combat. If the recommendations incorporated are carried out diligently, the fighter will have acquired a unique English working system.

Many oriental fighting systems exist and also work. Wherever you go they are practiced commonly but why be like a sheep in the common herd, dare to be different.

Why be a common sheep, when the Wolf mantle is yours for the taking?

A number of English Combat fighters competed with distincion resulting in two World Titles, for Sam Martin Jnr and Abby Steady

Single stick fight action from the 8th World Eskrima Kali Arnis World Championships 2004, Cebu, Philippines

CHAPTER I:
THE BASICS

This chapter will allow the fighter to progress through the first of the stages on the way to gaining proficiency in English Combat by explaining Part One of the Syllabus.

Now that you have become fit and are ready to start I will elaborate on the Part One basics.

Movement

First of all it is necessary to understand that in order to gain feedback in real time it is a requirement to practice all basics and combinations in the four parts with a training partner.

Stepping in is done by taking a full step forward with the rear foot and carrying out the attacking technique, with the rear arm from the on guard position.

Taking a full step back with the front foot does stepping back, and the rear arm carries out the blocking technique.

Always look at the top of your opponent's chest to achieve all over peripheral vision.

Blocks

The upper, inner, outer and inner-down blocks are carried out with the rear arm as the defender steps back.

The three-step move for each block is illustrated on the following pages. Follow the pictures from left to right:

Upper block:

Outer block:

Inner block:

Inner down block:

Brush block:

Press block:

Double press block:

The **snap punch** is carried out with the front fist and leg moving forward simultaneously. The punch is executed like all the punches in the system, with a double-piston movement. That is to say the punching fist moves forward, as the non-punching fist moves back: like the motion of a double-piston. This is common in many fighting systems and is very effective.

Darting-in techniques require both feet to move at the same time for speed. Fighters are advised to extend the punch by twisting the hip and turning the shoulder.

When darting in, try to imagine it as a jump forward with both feet at the same time. Try then to impact and focus just below the target surface area at the time when your body weight is going forward and slightly down.

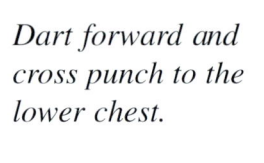

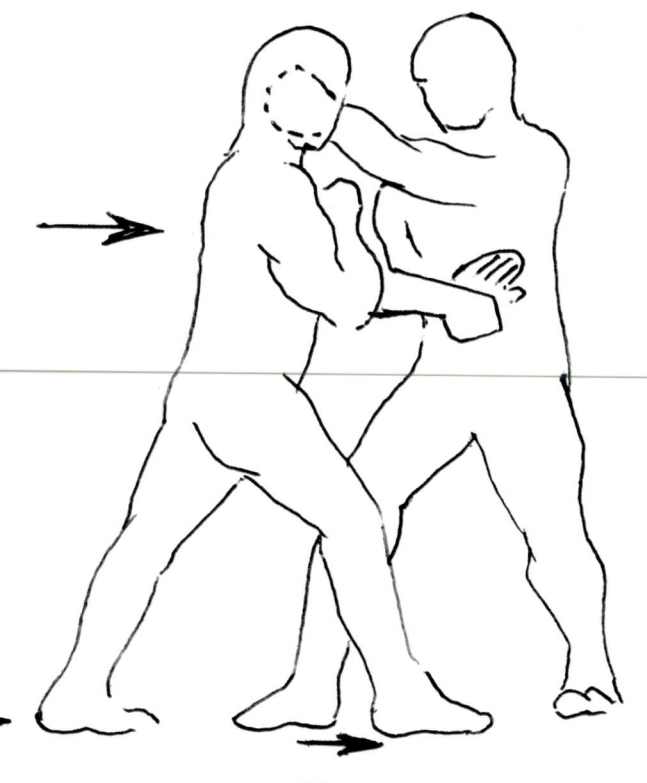

Dart forward and cross punch to the lower chest.

The defender should pivot on the front foot and slide the rear foot to the right.

Simultaneously blocking down and out with the right hand as a punch or back fist is executed to the attackers left eye.

CHAPTER I:
THE BASICS

Kicking

The English Combat system does not require fighters to demonstrate kicks any higher than the mid abdomen. In training it is recommended to kick to head height and develop the expertise and flexibility to do so. When you have trained to kick high you will have developed your body to accomplish a devastating low or mid high kick.

To pass the different parts, all kicks are no more than mid abdomen height.

Follow the illustrations below from left to right for each kick.

The **front kick** is executed using three consecutive moves:

The **roundhouse kick** is executed using three consecutive moves, which are illustrated below:

CHAPTER I:
THE BASICS

The **side kick** is executed using three consecutive moves, which are illustrated below:

Focus

Hitting or kicking with power is accomplished by the ability to generate and focus on a target with full body weight correctly applied, with relaxed speed.

Fully extending to focus point and then returning sharply, so that a penetrating force is applied, should complete all attacking techniques.

You should always try to complete the hit or kick about 2 inches below the surface on the target area. If you attempt to simply hit the surface you will only succeed in annoying your attacker instead of causing dismay or damage.

Aiming to complete the hit or kick with this focus will cause an explosive effect inside the body and can deter, if not destroy.

Practice on a hanging bag to develop good focus. If the bag swings when you impact on it you have done it incorrectly. All you have done is apply a push to the surface area. If the bag is bent and moves only a little, it is a good impact with focus.

When you have learned to recognize the feel of a good impact hit with focus, start training with focus mitts to improve speed of technique.

> It will take about three months to start to appreciate the points already stated in this chapter. In order to progress and develop, the fighter must study and practice all we have outlined until it becomes easy and natural to do.

Armed

Quarterstaff

In the armed segment of Part One you will find that it is necessary to be fully familiar with the angles of the English Broadsword Circle. The grip on the Quarterstaff and the body positioning is the two-thirds grip position. This is illustrated below:

When attacking you must use the angles and targets described and illustrated for the English Broadsword Circle.

See page 14

The illustrations below show the twelve strikes with the Quarterstaff, reading left-to-right starting with angle number one. After each strike return to the 'ready' position above:

CHAPTER I:
THE BASICS

Attack & Defence, 1-12

The blocking process is to step into the negative area of a strike, as illustrated below:

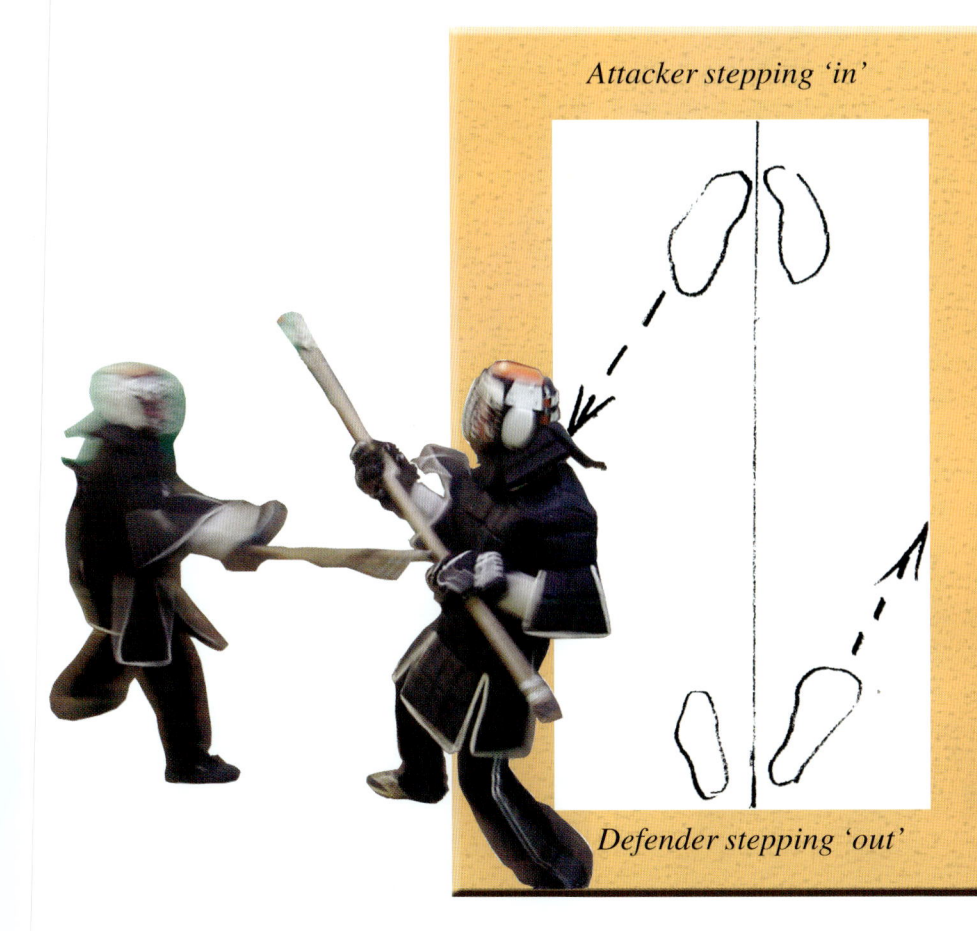

Attacker stepping 'in'

Defender stepping 'out'

If the defender stepped out to the left in this illustration then the attacker would be met and this would be a positive area move.

This would be useful if the defender wished to block the opponent by jamming but silly if stepping into a weapon.

The block is then the same strike as the attacker. For example, if I were to be attacked with the staff to angle number one, I would strike the same in return meaning that both staff will collide in mid strike effecting the block – see photo number 1 below.

The exceptions are the number three, four, five, six, nine, ten, eleven and twelve.

Follow the photographs from left to right. The attacker is on the right and strikes to each of the angles 1 – 12 in turn. Both fighters start from and return to the 'ready' position after each attack:

CHAPTER I: THE BASICS

CHAPTER 1:
THE BASICS

Knife

The knife attack and defence angles are the same as the Quarterstaff or Cudgel. The difference is that the fighter must first cut with the knife before blocking with the rear "live" hand. A cut and block is illustrated below (left to right):

Attack & Defence, 1-12

Follow the photographs from left to right. The attacker is on the right and strikes to each of the angles 1 – 12 in turn. Each photo shows the final position of the defender having cut first then blocked with the live hand. Both fighters start from and return to the 'ready' position after each attack:

32

CHAPTER I:
THE BASICS

Combinations

Unarmed

The unarmed combinations include the basic techniques already explained except they are practiced and then demonstrated at this stage as a flowing fluid combination. The fighter will need to start by adopting the basic on-guard and return to the same while maintaining the appropriate defence throughout.

The fighter must try and establish focus for each and every technique instead of relying upon the last one in a charge forward. The forward momentum, however, must be carried out with shocking alacrity.

The Front Punch

Adopting the on-guard and stepping forward with the rear leg, the fighter punches with the rear fist, pulling back with the forward arm to cover the right side of the jaw.

The Snap Punch

Adopting the on-guard, the fighter swiftly extends the front foot and fist forward, snapping the punch sharply into the target.

The Cross Punch

Adopting the on-guard, the fighter punches with the rear fist while turning the rear hip forward. The rear knee is relaxed and the front fist is brought sharply back to cover the right side of the jaw.

Armed

The armed combinations are again completed with a partner who will act as the attacker who is in retreat.

The fighter will start in the basic on-guard position to commence the combination and return to the same on conclusion. Appropriate defensive posture must be shown throughout and on completion.

The crouch shown at the end of the first combination is taken from old English bowing carried out in deference to a Lady.

The eyes can see forward and back simultaneously

The hand doffing the hat can loose it and grasp the sword hilt

The feet allow a spin to face rearward

To bow in front of a Lady, while doffing one's cap, was not just a process of good manners, it allowed the gentleman access to his sword and the ability to turn speedily if required. It was not unknown for Ladies to use their standing and charms to be rid of competition or adversaries at Court. A gentleman was most vulnerable bowing and in doing so could be risking his life. The elaborate bowing affected gave the man a good chance of survival. Consider the bow and the options as illustrated above.

The two armed combinations are simple to carry out.

Combination One
No 1 double arc, No 4 snap hit and double circle (show footwork).

Adopt the on-guard; execute two consecutive number one strikes, snap out and back to number four. This is shown in the following photo sequence.

CHAPTER I:
THE BASICS

Glover Family English Combat Fighting System

TERRY GLOVER'S TRAINING TIPS

To fire combinations in real life effectively, practice them with alacrity with a training partner at any opportunity, without warning.

Next, from the on-guard, move back one pace starting with the forward foot and as you do so you must execute a circular strike number twelve, then repeat. End up as the illustration for the bow, except head up, facing forward and have the stick in the right hand at shoulder level pointing the butt out to the opponent at your face height.

35

CHAPTER I: THE BASICS

Have your left hand in front of your chest, palm facing the opponent.

Now practice until swift in execution.

CHAPTER I:
THE BASICS

Combination Two

No 1 then No 2, thrust No 5, fan, strike No 8 then thrust No 9.

Adopt the on-guard; strike number one and two, then thrust to number five. Draw up the striking arm to perform a **fan strike** commencing on the left side of the opponent's temple with a reverse hit.

See the following diagrams:

Use the free hand to check distance to the opponent by touching and lean back to effectively hit your target either side of the head.

Rotate the weapon-holding arm to hit on the opponent's left temple then right and end on the left side, thereby executing three rapid fan strikes.

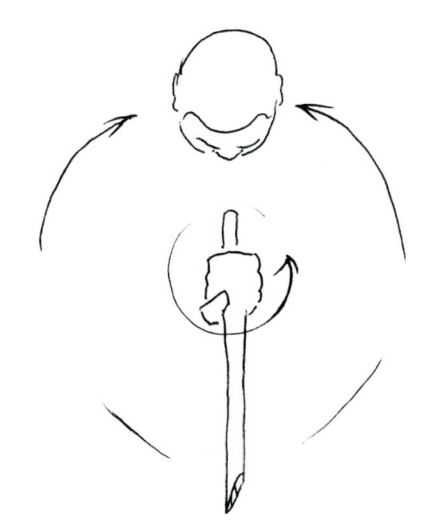

From the last reverse strike to the temple, draw back the hand to strike at number eight and thrust nine.

Adopt the on-guard, practice until swift.

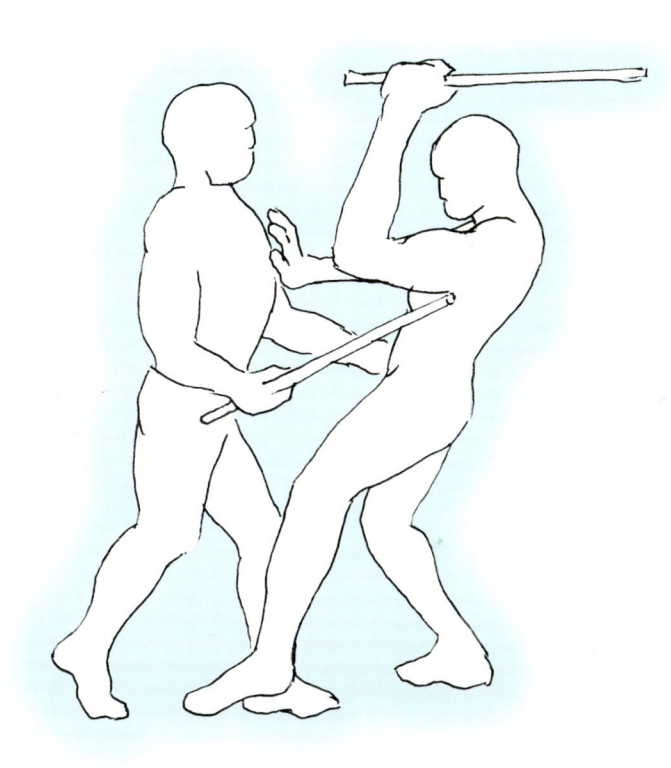

TERRY GLOVER'S TRAINING TIPS

Practice your fanning skills by holding two sticks, striking one with the other. This can be done without a training partner. Practice vertical and horizontal fanning.

CHAPTER I:
THE BASICS

Although fighting more than one person at a time is foolhardy and dangerous, there may be occasions when you have no choice if attacked.

The only way to find out safely what it is like, is to train different scenarios and deliberate upon them collectively.

CHAPTER II:
TAKEDOWNS

This chapter will outline the extra skills necessary to advance, now that the basics are becoming second nature. Daily practice is necessary, as with all physical skills.

Unarmed

In this part the fighter now progresses to the takedowns from the blocks. Each block can be used to effect taking your attacker to the ground. These takedowns are extremely simple and therefore of magnificent value in combat. Follow the photos below from left to right:

One:

This one is done after blocking a high strike. In photos 3, 4 and 5 the defender keeps the right foot in one place and circles anticlockwise with the left foot to affect the takedown.

39

Two:

After receiving a punch aimed to the middle body, pull the arm straight and towards you to effect the takedown.

Three:

This is again after an attack to middle body.

After lifting the attacker's arm on photo three, place right foot in and left foot around in a circle anticlockwise to effect the actual takedown.

Four:

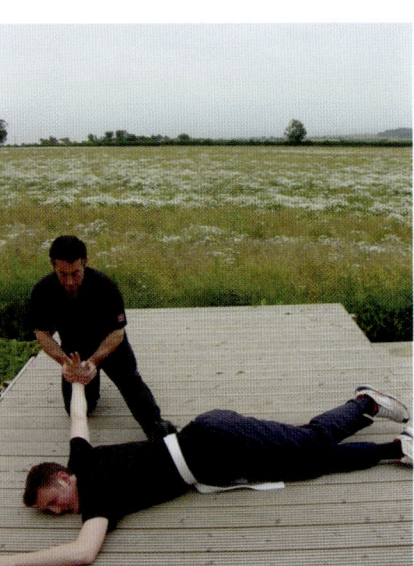

In photo four (going from left to right) the defender once again pulls back and down to affect the takedown.

The way the entire movement is accomplished is smoothly, with only as much strength as necessary to complete.

If the grip is correct the attacker will succumb without effort.

Notice that the left foot is pressing against the attackers body to stop from turning over and releasing the hold or starting a counter.

Always remember that if the attacker is a trained fighter they will attempt a counter so you must finish with an arrest hold or disabling strike.

Five:

Sometimes an opponent will not actually step forward and will simply snap a punch out towards you in either a feint or determined hit. The above illustration shows the counter to a sudden attack.

Please note that it is difficult indeed to carry this out and only the well trained will be able to pull it off. The reason is that the feint or strike from the front fist is extremely fast and difficult to see coming. It is emphasized therefore that all fighters concentrate upon their fitness, distance and timing drills to a good level of expertise before attempting this counter.

When the knee strike is carried out the defender must point the toes down to allow the point of the knee to contact with the attackers face. Failure to do this will mean only the padded quadriceps will make the impact and let the attacker off.

At the same time the knee strikes, the defender should also pull down on the attackers head to increase the effect of the blow.

CHAPTER II:
TAKEDOWNS

Six:

This sequence shows how you can sweep an opponent even if your legs are damaged in combat. In schools and in the street, children learn to do this sweep in play fighting but leave it behind once they become adults. This is a pity as all skills learned in catch as catch can games become useful as an adult.

It is necessary to note that before this sweep or any other damaging technique is used, there must be a distraction of some kind, maybe a punch or a kick, a finger strike to the eyes, even a shout or scream.

I have met precious few opponents that would allow me to hurt them without putting up a stiff resistance.

Try and recall days as a child pressing your knees behind a friends knees to tumble them in high spirits. Recall how good it felt to be able to accomplish this with ease and be the toast of your fellows. Then remember that to manage this you had to first practice over and over for many weeks, then realize you must do the same again.

CHAPTER II:
TAKEDOWNS

Seven:

To sweep an opponent that has attempted a kick is difficult to do. There are many ways to accomplish this but you must try to master one or two that you can carry out instinctively well, rather than have an arsenal of thirty that only occasionally work.

Remember that an opponent who is a good kicker can drop you with a well-placed kick unless you practice techniques against them continuously.

During your training sessions, arrange to spend some time defending only. It is easier to attack, than defend, so if you can competently defend yourself first, then attacking becomes routinely efficient.

Ask your training colleague to attack you continuously and try to anticipate a kick during the combinations. Your opponent may show intention to kick by the shoulders leaning forward, sometimes backwards or by making distance to achieve the kick.

**CHAPTER II:
TAKEDOWNS**

Eight:

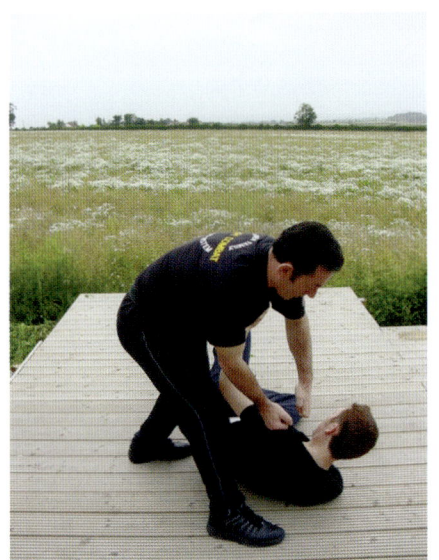

This sequence is admirably completed but note that the fifth photo looking left to right showing the foot sweep, can only be efficiently done by lifting the body weight in order to do so.

A sidekick can be swift and too powerful to stop or scoop with an arm. An arm versus a leg will always end with the leg as the victor.

Practice this often and use only when sure of success.

Study these moves well, disregard them at your peril.

Armed

Holding it in the original English on-guard, we now use the **Quarterstaff** at this stage. The Quarterstaff is first held by the right hand with palm uppermost and the Quarterstaff grasped in the balanced middle. This is half way up the entire length. Then it is grasped by the left hand to the left of right and half way from the butt to the right hand. In other words, a quarter of the length. You now are holding the Quarterstaff correctly. Now step with the right leg forward and knee slightly bent and place your hands in the basic on guard.

This is illustrated as follows:

Holding the Quarterstaff in this way enables the fighter to utilize it's ability to take on attackers at long range as well as short range when held in the two thirds grip learned in part one. The English Broadsword Circle is brought into play again and the same footwork is used.

Here we also have a new type of training, which is the **block and counter**. Working with a training partner the first person attacks and makes a strike along one of the numbered angles. The attacking strike is blocked and a counter is affected. While practising the block and counter and demonstrating it when progressing through the levels the fighter must use a variety of heights including fighting from the floor, moving circular as well as linear. A critical observer would look for good use of the live or rear hand when close in and the ability to recover balance with fluidity and grace.

The **Short staff** or Cudgel is now used at long, medium and close range to show the effectiveness at all ranges. We learn to use the point and butt as well as striking, slicing and thrusting. The range drill is simple to carry out but hard to keep going for any length of time in practice. It is however very important in the development of the fighter in this system.

The long, medium and short range is carried out in quick succession. The fighters are advised to look, not into the eyes of their training partner but at the top of the chest, which allows for being able to see around the entire body and will warn easily of movement anywhere. This is applied throughout the fighting process regardless of being armed or unarmed. Always keep your eyes on the top of the chest to allow adequate peripheral vision.

CHAPTER II:
TAKEDOWNS

The Long-range drill

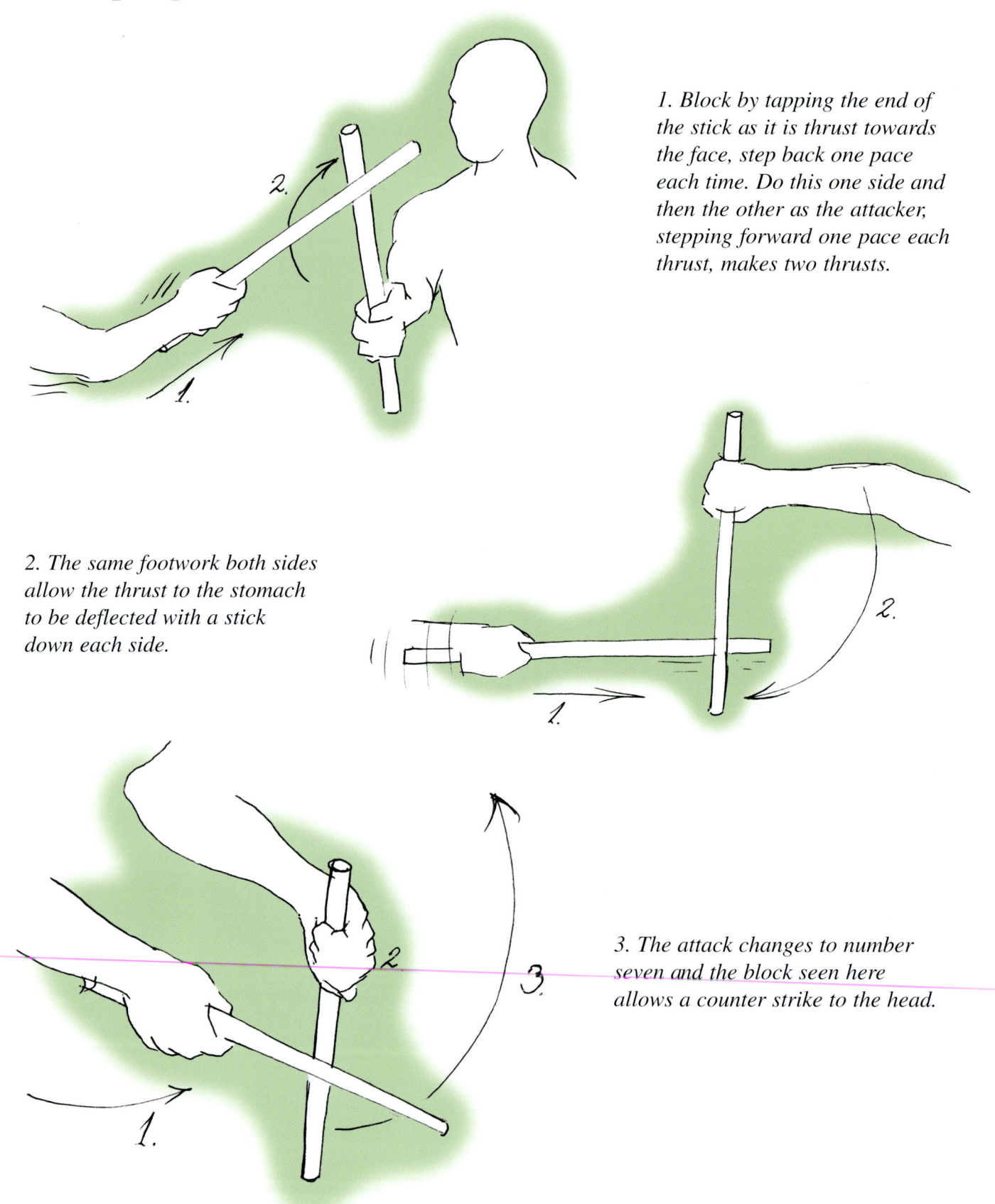

1. Block by tapping the end of the stick as it is thrust towards the face, step back one pace each time. Do this one side and then the other as the attacker, stepping forward one pace each thrust, makes two thrusts.

2. The same footwork both sides allow the thrust to the stomach to be deflected with a stick down each side.

3. The attack changes to number seven and the block seen here allows a counter strike to the head.

CHAPTER II: TAKEDOWNS

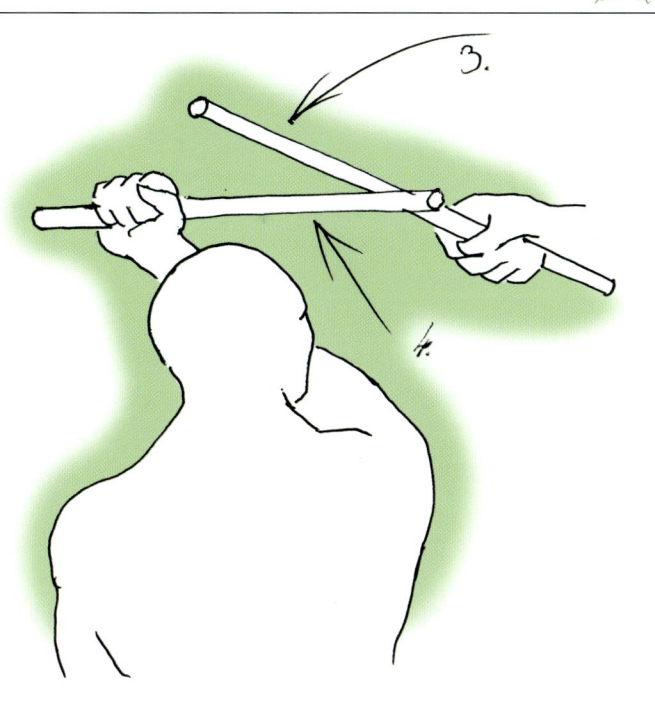

4. The attack is countered and a strike to number eleven is made as shown. The sequence continues with a number seven strike.

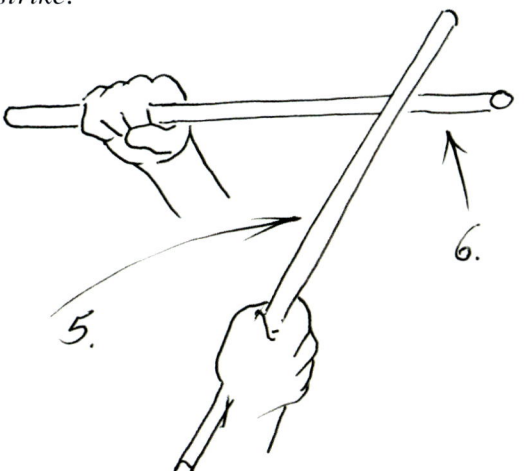

The Medium-range drill

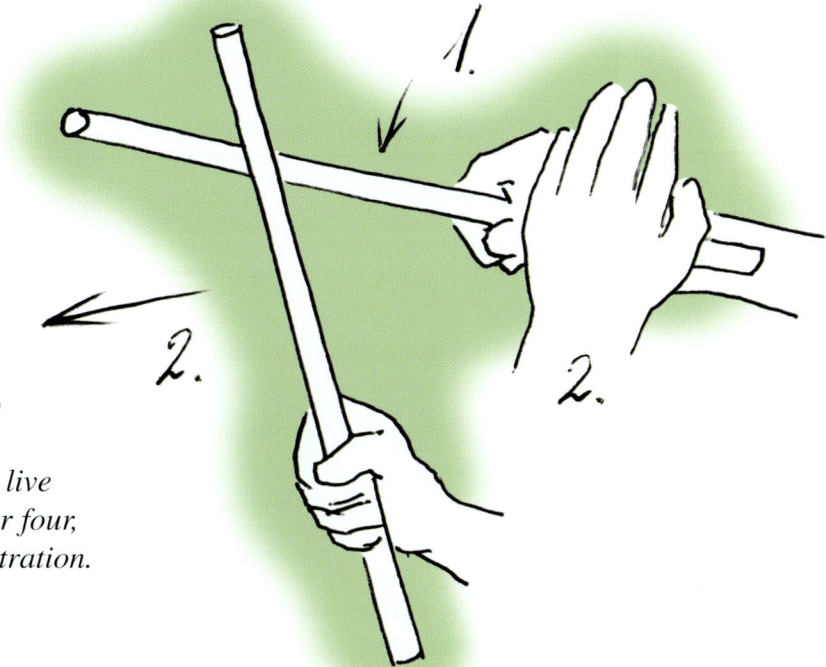

1. After practice, a strike is made to number one instead of seven and is blocked by the stick followed by the live hand. This allows a strike to number four, which is blocked as in the next illustration.

CHAPTER II: TAKEDOWNS

2. The block is executed as shown with both hands simultaneously. The stick hand of the blocker draws back and comes forward to form a thrust to number five.

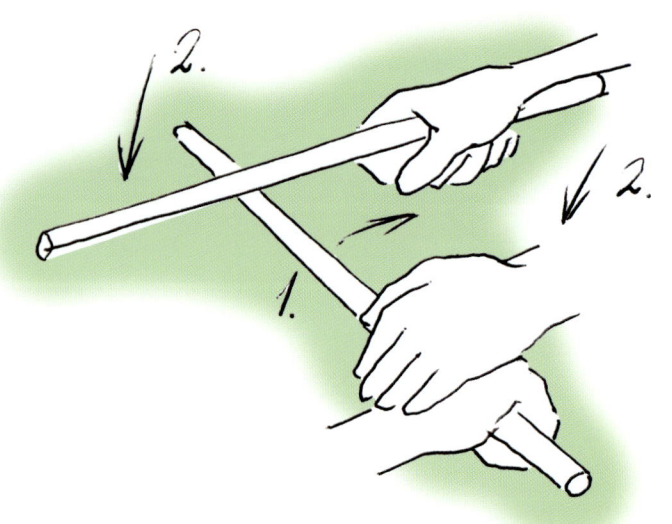

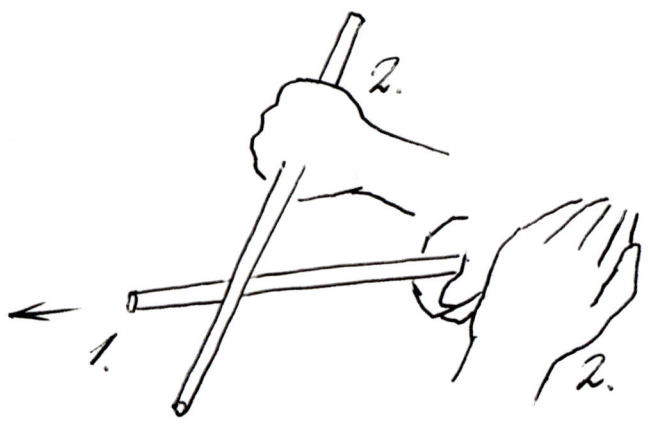

3. The thrust to number five is blocked with the right hand and checked with the left. As the stick is down it allows a strike to number twelve.

4. The number twelve strike is blocked and countered with a number seven.

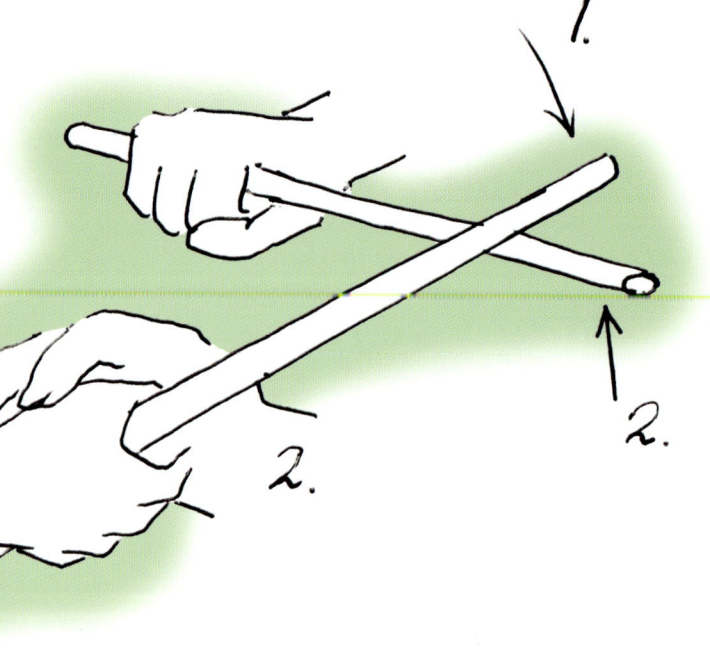

CHAPTER II:
TAKEDOWNS

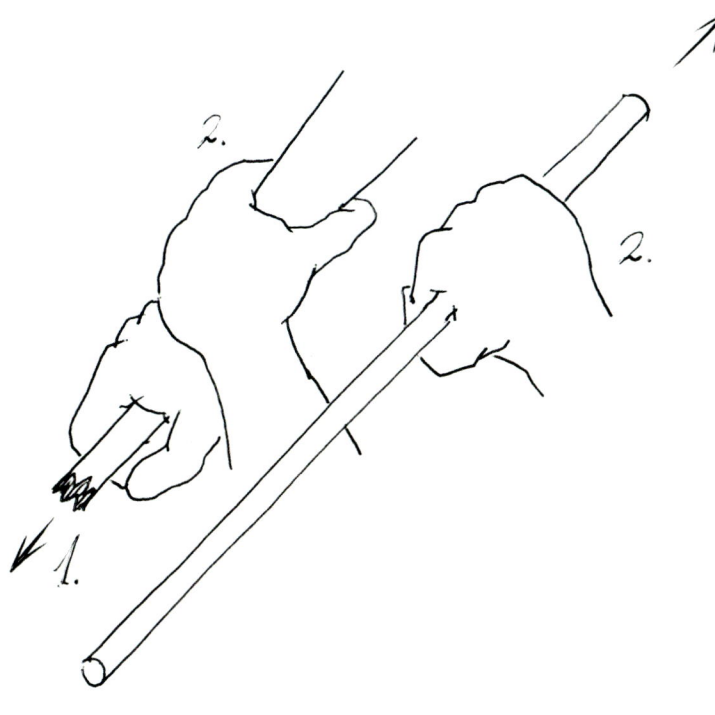

5. The number seven strike is checked and a butt strike to the face ensues.

6. The butt strike is checked with the left hand and the striker then strikes number twelve by rotating the checked stick overhand.

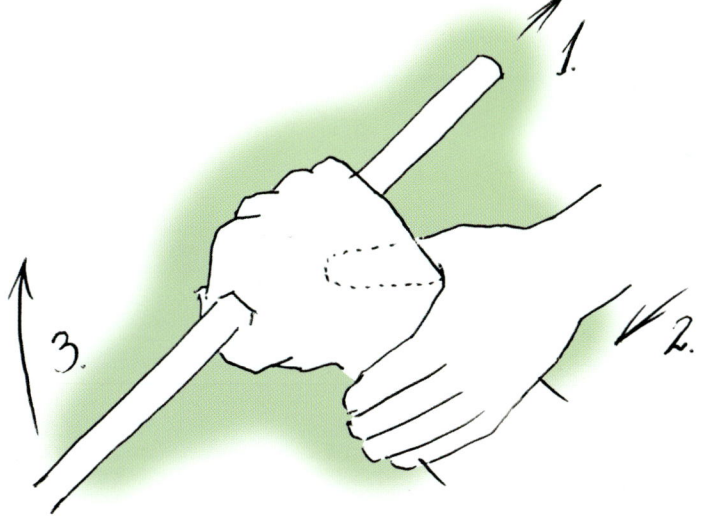

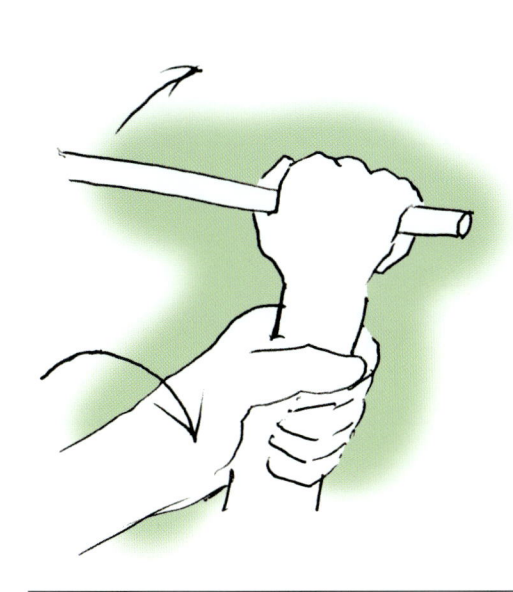

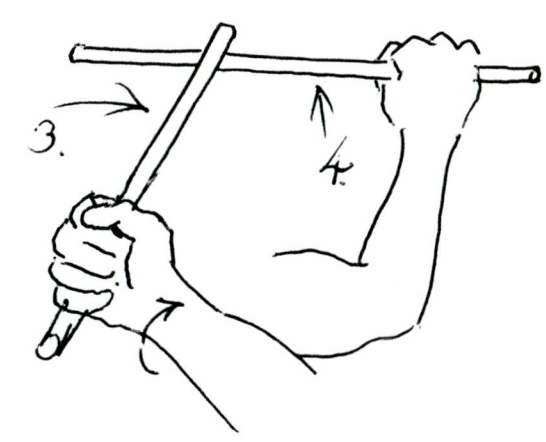

7. The right stick hand in reverse posture blocks the number twelve rotated strike and is in turn grasped and pulled down in a semi-circle, deflected and the number seven strike continues the sequence.

CHAPTER II:
TAKEDOWNS

The Short-range drill

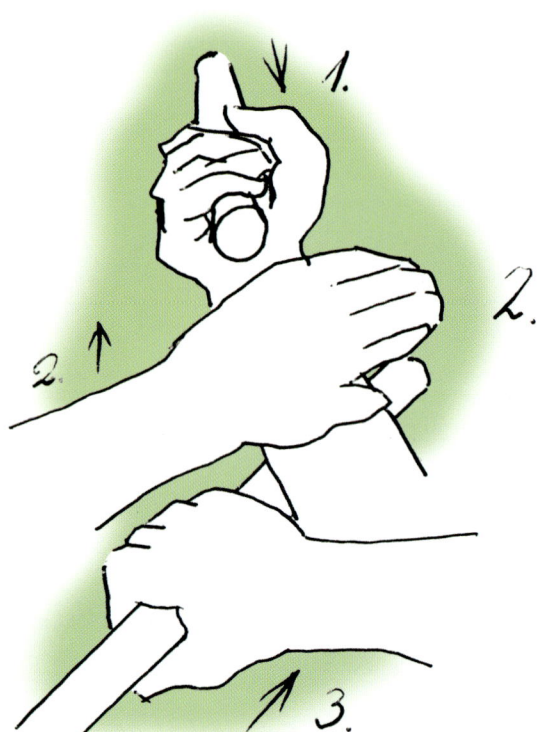

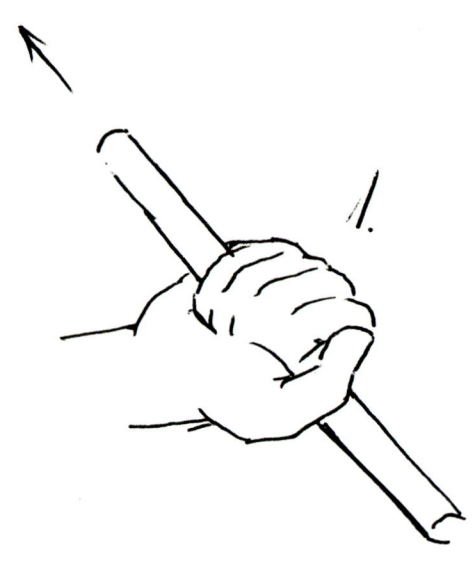

1. To go to the next stage the attacker now attacks the face with the butt instead of number seven, as above.

This is blocked and hooked as in the illustration on the left. The hooking stick bringing the arm and stick down in a semi-circle.

The defender then starts the sequence again by striking with the butt to face as above.

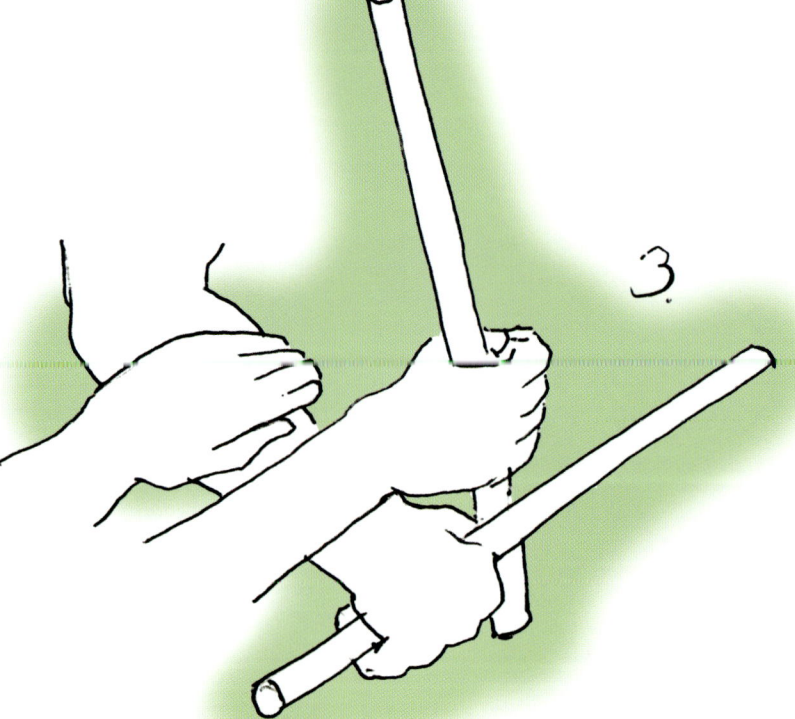

CHAPTER II:
TAKEDOWNS

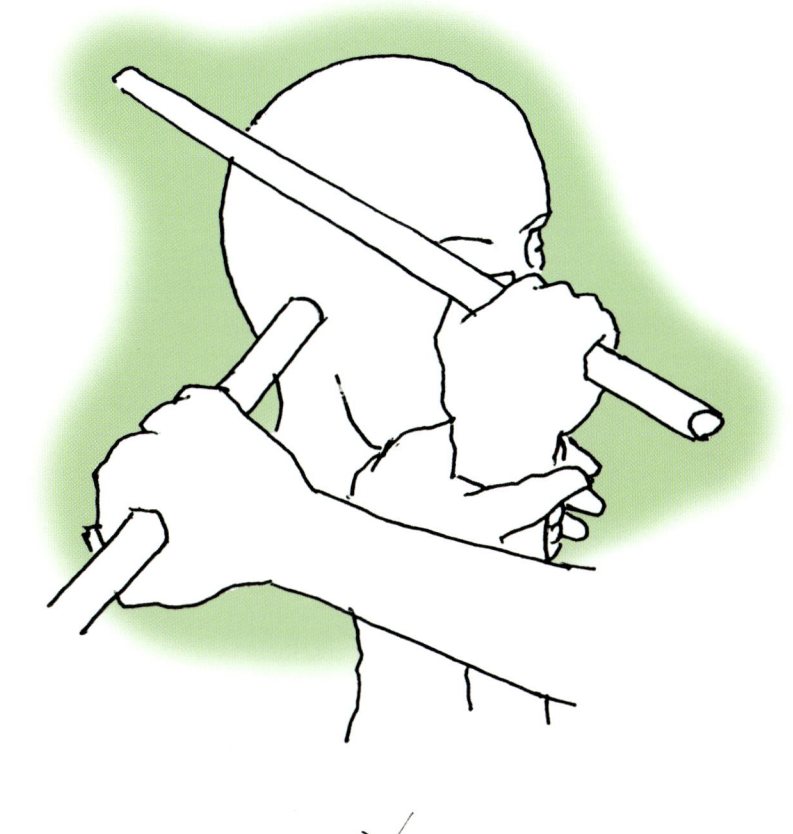

2. After practising the above drill the sequence is again changed by passing the attacking butt with the left hand and striking to the temple with the stick.

This is dealt with by checking with the left hand and striking to the ribs, where a forearm completes the blocking sequence.

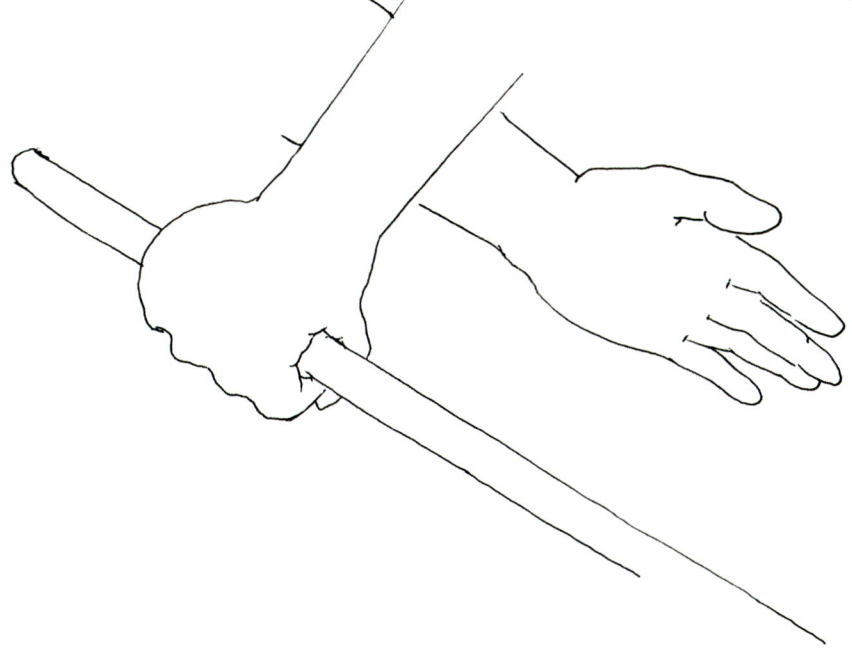

TERRY GLOVER'S TRAINING TIPS

To become good with a cudgel, pick one up and play with it often to develop a feel for the weapon.

CHAPTER II: TAKEDOWNS

Knife Stripping

The knife in part two is used to practice stripping, which is the ability to take away or disarm an attacker armed with a knife.

The twelve strips are effected simply and are illustrated below, left to right:

The above illustrations show how to disarm attacks coming to angles one, nine and eleven with blocking hand palm up, three and seven, palm down.

The last illustration shows that when the knife is grasped, it cannot be with a grip that goes around the blade, as that will cut you. The pressure is executed with the palm pad and flat grip along the blade side.

As hand contact is made with the knife, the knife disarm is effected, by a popping motion, of part push with the knife contact and part pull with the grip on the hand.

Spontaneous Explosive Alacrity

Understand the above three words well and what they mean when used together. You will then understand how to respond to an attacker armed with a blade.

CHAPTER II: TAKEDOWNS

Above is shown the grip on the knife to remove it from the attacker's grasp. Practice this many times.

The above illustrations show how to disarm from angles two, four, eight and twelve. The difference is one of **height** - the lower the attack, the lower your posture is required to be - see below:

The elbow is used to roll the arm and place the hand in a position to grasp and turn the arm into an arm lock or submission.

Block and counter with the knife is similar to that with the Cudgel except you must slice with the knife first on the wrist of the attacker or training partner with your blunted training blade then use the live or rear hand to effect the tap block. Using the live hand flat palm to strike and cause the attacking hand to be stopped momentarily carries out the tap block. The fighters must realise that to grasp the knife hand instead of tapping will cause a dangerous practice in the training hall and in real combat.

DO NOT DO IT!

Combinations

Unarmed

The combinations in Part Two on page 125 allow for development of the basics into flowing techniques again. The fighters must strive to attain good focus and alacrity.

Use flowing combinations more reminiscent of dancers than stuttering robots.

Unarmed combinations here will include a step up technique not yet encountered so far in Par One of the Syllabus.

This is the step up front kick: Adopting the basic right guard first, then to affect the kick, one simply brings the back foot up alongside the front, and then kicks using the original forward leg. Fluidity is necessary here and the aim will be to move forward adroitly, catching the attacker stumbling backwards trying to avoid your forward attacking momentum.

The back fist is carried out by springing forward, aiming to connect a rear arm elbow strike with the opponent's nose. The arm is then extended to make the fist connect to the side of the head landing upon the temple or the orbit of the eye.

When trying to impact your elbow into the opponent's nose, you will notice that he will move his head back to avoid it. This is not a problem as you can now land your back fist blow cleanly upon the side of his head, as it is now at the correct range.

If you manage to catch your opponent off guard and actually strike with the elbow first then so be it. It means your training has been good and you are moving quicker than him.

It must be mentioned at this point that an elbow strike landing upon the head will cause the skin to split. The splitting skin will start blood streaming down the face. This will mean that your opponent will be temporarily blinded with his own blood. Take advantage of this and strike once more to drop your attacker in his tracks and make him think again about attacking someone.

Armed

A new **Quarterstaff** drill is introduced at this stage, which is a **twirling drill**. You will see it done when the Bandmaster of a Military Band is marching at the front twirling and rolling his staff. These moves are taken from old traditional Quarterstaff training sequences.

In order to achieve flow and dexterity with this amazing weapon, one must practice drills such as these. There are many twirling drills available. The simple way to learn them is by looking around for a person that is doing cheerleading or band leading and has already acquired these twirling skills.

The **cudgel** training is accelerated now with the learning of **the rap**. This is used mainly at close quarters and is highly effective at demoralising and providing opportunities for disarms. The rap is done by backhanding the attacker with the cudgel low and high one side, strike across the knees to then strike low and high the other side. The turning motion of the body gives the fighter the ability to disarm more effectively.

The **cut and thrust** mentioned here in Part Two is block and counter with the **knife** but the knife is also used point down as well as point up. The point up is simply for long range and point down for close-in. Practice at this gives alarming abilities with a blade. The critical observer must look for all previous mentioned points and now to also include the hooking possibilities of the knife, point down.

Hooking can tie up an opponent ready to take him down, as well as cutting and thrusting upwards.

Light Sparring

Light sparring is unarmed and semi-contact. The two fighters are demonstrating the ability to fight unarmed but not to include grappling or takedowns at this stage. Padding on the fists and feet with a groin guard are advised here. All the unarmed blocks, punches and kicks should be demonstrated with fluidity. Two fighters taking part should be refereed as detailed later in this book.

To prepare for unarmed sparring it is necessary to train with pads held by a training partner, which will allow the fighter to actually land blows with full power and not hurt himself or his training partner in the execution.

This also allows the fighter to get feedback on his strikes to sense whether they are landing with full power and good technique.

THRUSTS & FOOTSWEEPS

Move forward, with the left hand checking the opponent's attacking weapon hand. Place the left leg behind the opponent's leading leg and thrust into his ribs with the point.

Turn your hips so that you are facing away, and slide your foot sharply forward, finishing with a thrust to ribs once more.

Alternatively, simply check the attacker's weapon hand and strike to the face with the butt of your stick...

Both sequences here show that a swift thrust into body or face can stop an attack...

CHAPTER III:
RELEASES

In this chapter the fighter is introduced to releases. The process of releasing is necessary to escape an attackers grip. The way to become good at doing it is to practice many times. The different releases are illustrated as follows:

One:

Make and complete the circle fluidly with no jerking at all. Use little strength and rely upon the technique to accomplish the release.

Two:

Rest the elbow on your hip for leverage.

Three:

When practicing move number three, the fighter must carry out the practice at speed, relaxed, and while the opponent is gripping realistically.

Initially it is necessary to step forward to make the opponents grip become relaxed to affect the release. Pretend that his grip is working.

Practice this at home and outside, as well as in your training area. Real life experience shows that you can be grabbed anywhere and at anytime.

Four:

Once the circular movement is at its top height, move in to your attacker with your body as your hands descend to complete the circular movement.

61

**CHAPTER III:
RELEASES**

Five:

Pinch the upper under arm viciously between thumb and curled index fingers.

Six:

Do not turn your head to complete this move, as doing so will twist your neck in the attackers grasp, which is painful.

Seven:

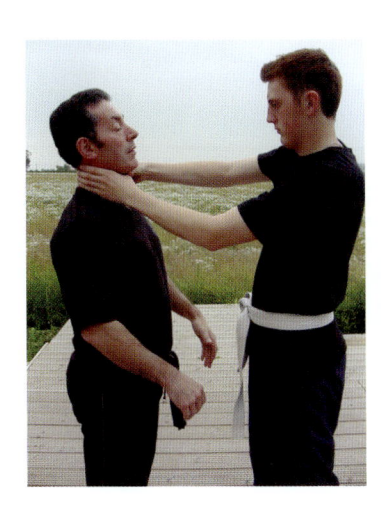

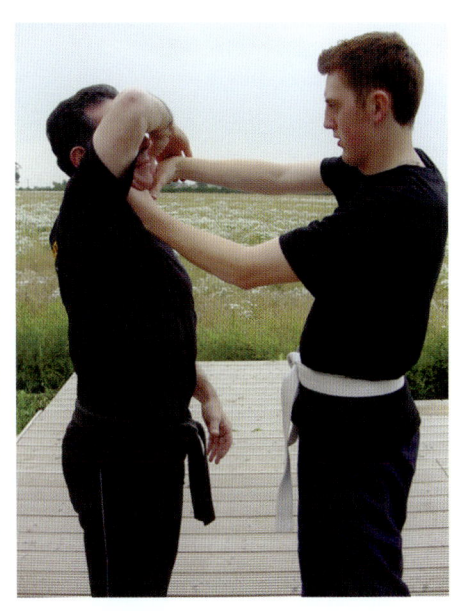

Move your body in to the attacker as you grip his hand.

Eight:

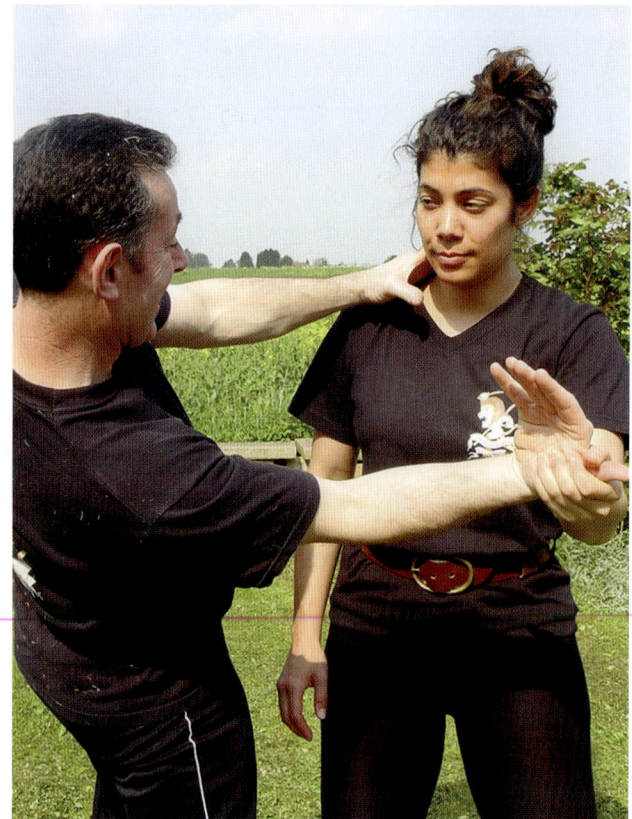

Use your uninvolved hand to increase pressure if the attacker is resisting.

Nine:

Move your body in to the attacker to make the initial grip.

Ten:

Strike the attacker's chin hard.

**CHAPTER III:
RELEASES**

Eleven:

When carrying out number eleven it will be necessary to use good speed in implementation to stand a chance of pulling it off.

All of these breakaway moves from a strangle hold have been deliberately laid out in stages to show how it is done. Please do not attempt them in real life at a slow speed. As with all other techniques, these moves must be practiced. It is also prudent to use a disabling blow, or strike, at commencement.

CHAPTER III:
RELEASES

Twelve:

Impact hard on the elbows of the attacker as if pushing his arms to a single point.

Thirteen:

Open your hands and allow all your fingers to spread and find a suitable target on the face where it is painful. There are many of them.

Fourteen:

Grab and pull the testicles, do not hit them, as some men show no pain when that is done.

Fifteen:

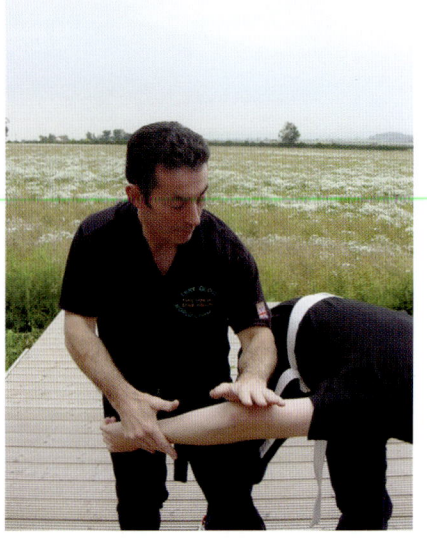

Move your body in to your attacker to make this move possible.

68

**CHAPTER III:
RELEASES**

Attacking for Defence

When attacking a person it is necessary to know which technique to use on which part of the body. If a fighter uses a punch to strike an attacker's head it can be counterproductive. The head is extremely hard and contains much bone. It is a genetic marvel that is designed by Mother Nature to absorb blows and keep going. You do not need to take my advice on this. Simply watch a boxing match. How many punches can they take to the head? I rest my case.

In English Combat it is appropriate to strike with **hard weapons to soft targets**. Instead of punching to the head, consider punching to the **throat**. Instead of punching to the muscular or distended stomach, punch to the **groin**. If you are in possession of a weapon, then you can hit **bone**. A blow to the collarbone with a Cudgel, Quarterstaff or axe, is a marvelous way to stop an attacker. Try to always have the upper hand and do not injure yourself on your attacker *(that is very silly!)*.

Target areas used in English Combat are extremely simple to learn. Imagine someone has hit you on your own body somewhere, would it hurt you? If the answer is no, then forget it as a potential target. If the answer is yes, then remember it and use it on an attacker.

There are occasions when you may decide to **contain or arrest an attacker** instead of knocking him down or out. This system shows you ways to do this and advocates practice once again. It is wise to note at this stage that when a move is referred to as a lock it is exactly that, and when in training they should be applied lightly and the training partner should endeavor not to struggle too strongly whilst it is being applied. If a lock is too tight or hurting, then the fighter must signal this by tapping out to acquiesce.

The shoulder strike and buttocks strike are illustrated here. Do these slowly in practice. Have respect for human life. These moves are dangerous.

69

**CHAPTER III:
RELEASES**

The shoulder strike and buttocks strike are taught to disable an attacker. They should be practiced gently on a human being and only strongly on a hanging bag.

Be Warned – They work

Focus

The principle of straight line and centre line striking will allow the fighter to accomplish placing full **body weight** on to a simple technique. To carry this out the body weight is propelled forward, generated by the hip and legs. The technique is central to the fighter's body, and focus will carry the body weight through the target. This is illustrated below:

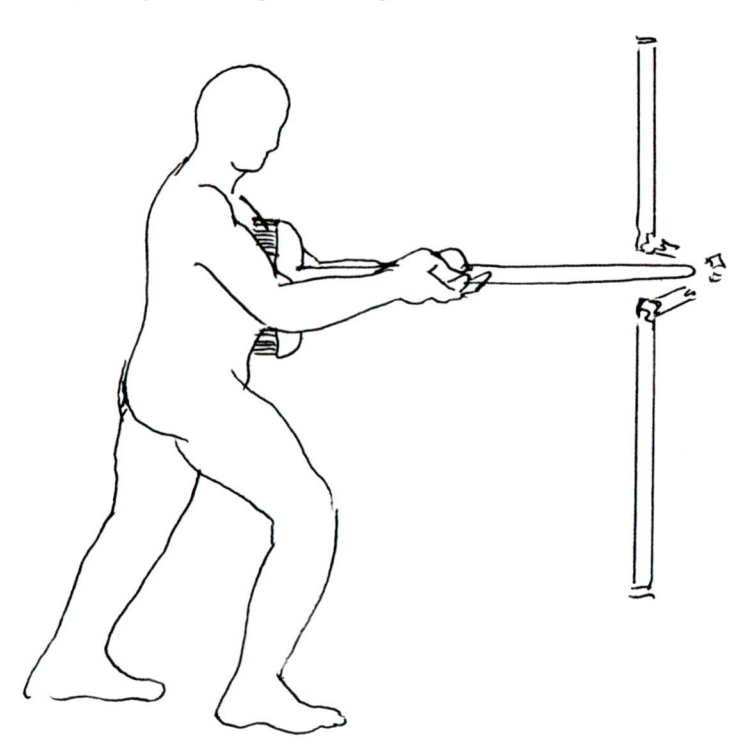

See this work for yourself by copying the illustration.

The point of the broom is your focus point. Place all energy and body weight on this point.

Notice that the more you practice, the less effort you need for great effect, as long as there is focus.

This principle holds true for all weapons and the human body in attack.

Practice Focus with relaxed speed.

When practicing to focus on a point to strike, you must aim to penetrate about 2 inches below the surface to achieve a shock effect. If you aim to land a blow or technique on the surface itself, the force will dissipate easily before maximum effect is achieved.

The way to see this done commonly is to attend a simple boxing bout and watch the fighters. You will notice that each boxer will strike while exhaling quickly, doing this will allow the force of the blow to travel through, instead of land on, the target.

Focusing and breathing properly also allow the fighter to throw combinations and absorb blows if they miss. If you are already breathing out you will tense muscles and have a musculature ready to accept an impact without damage.

**CHAPTER III:
RELEASES**

To make sure you land a blow with sufficient shock impact to break bone and separate muscle fibres it is necessary to practice sometimes with hanging objects.

I take time to do focus-specific training, this means that I hang various objects on string around my training area and try to break them without making them swing afterwards.

Do not hang pieces of metal, as that would be silly. Hang long pieces of wood about two to three feet long.

As a school child it used to be popular in simple science to demonstrate the force of air pressure. A wooden rule was placed half on the edge of the table, then a sheet of paper was placed on top. If sufficient speed was used to break the rule with a sharp blow without disturbing the sheet of paper (like punching or kicking an opponent), then it ably demonstrated that air pressure was resisting the upward movement of the paper slowing it down. The greater the speed of the blow, the greater the air pressure, allowing the rule to be broken.

This is also the principle of focus; therefore, it should be learned and understood.

Weapon sequences are to be practiced in order to demonstrate competence, and are deliberately carried out at one-minute intervals. The reason for this is simple. A human being can go at full speed for about forty-five seconds and then lactic acid in the muscles slows you down. A fighter needs to be able to fight using successive combinations on one or more opponents. To make the best use of this knowledge it is wise to train always to last for at least one minute at full speed. You get used to drawing reserves from stored glycogen in the blood stream. It is a process that is felt: when you reach the point at which you cannot go on, speed up! Eventually you will learn to recognize this feeling and make use of it. Many times in competition I have fought fighters who were just as fast or faster than me. It did not matter because when they started to slow down I was speeding up. No contest. It is commonly recognised as a process whereby all around you seem to be moving in slow motion while you are moving normally.

It must be said at this point that it is only through sheer bloody guts when doing your roadwork and bag work that the body is prepared for this. Always in training, use differing routines and constantly surprise the body. It does not take long for the body to get used to even amazingly stressful routines. You must push yourself to achieve ever-greater physical accomplishments. Now and again, relax, have a couple of days off, then start again. The human being lives for stress, thrives on stress and needs stress to realise it is alive. Stress that it can deal with that is, not stress that cannot be alleviated, as that is harmful.

After a hard workout you will receive chemicals from your own brain that will boost the 'feel good' factor in you. Making you feel good to be alive.

CHAPTER III:
RELEASES

Unarmed Combat

Example unarmed technique in three parts – attacker on the right, defender on the left.

The simultaneous block and uppercut to the jaw:

Start on guard and the attacker snaps a punch with the lead fist to the face of the defender.

The defender moves forward as he blocks with his lead hand brushing the attacking fist to one side.

The defender simultaneously strikes with an uppercut from the rear hand, dropping the attacker.

CHAPTER IV:
WEAPONS SKILLS - INCLUDING DISARMS

The Whip

In this chapter we see how the whip is introduced into the syllabus ready to accomplish part four. The whip used can be six or eight feet and is a bullwhip or stock-whip. There is only a nominal difference between the two. The bullwhip is preferable to be used at medium to long range, with limited skills at close quarters and the stock whip has ability at all ranges. I like to use a bullwhip myself, as it is more of a challenge.

The two basic cracks and multiple hitting are illustrated below:

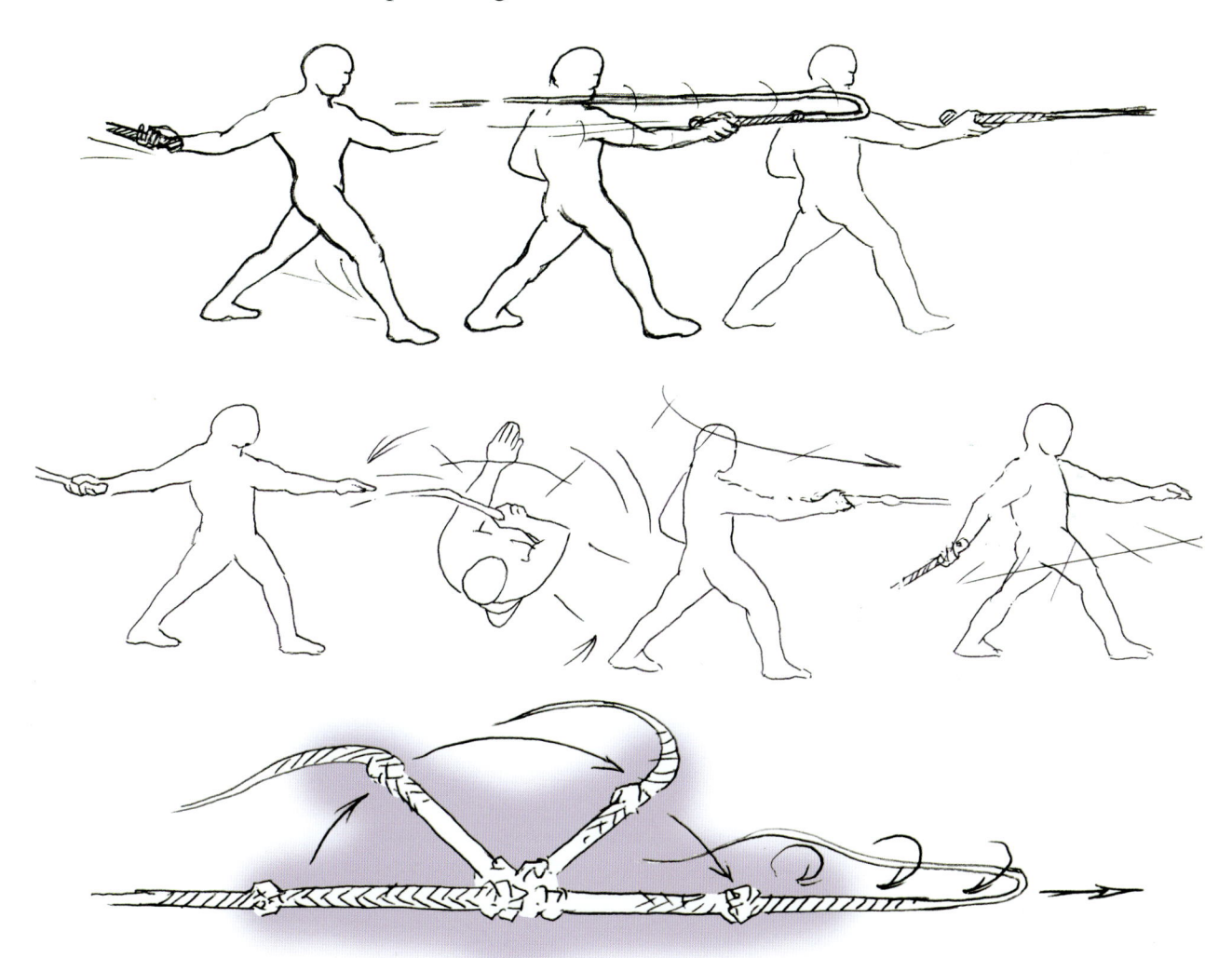

As the whip is thrown forward, the grip is twisted through 180 degrees, which allows the weapon to uncurl from the heavy handle outwards. The end of the whip uncurls at over 700mph. Please do not aim at living things in practice.

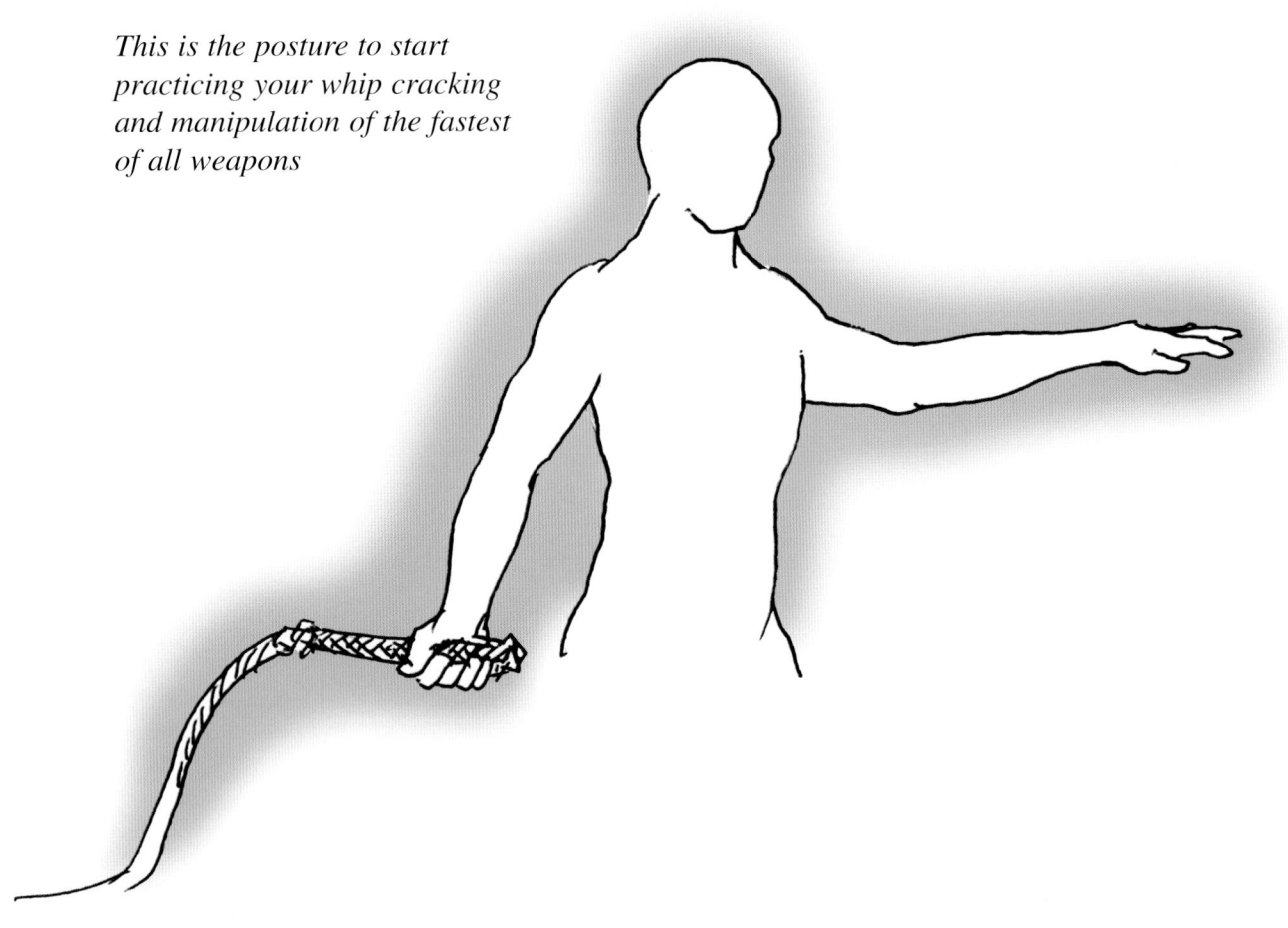

This is the posture to start practicing your whip cracking and manipulation of the fastest of all weapons

To acquire multiple hitting abilities, the fighter must start as above and execute one strike.

The strike is carried out by uncurling the whip with force straight through the target with one to two inches of the end of the weapon penetrating like a punch.

Maintain the forward impact by following through with the weapon holding hand.

Allow the weapon to go around your head to the left, forward and down to your right.

When the change in direction occurs, the impact on to the target with the end of the weapon must take place.

Practice this many times and then start to change direction until proficient at any attack angle in any combination or single strike.

Vary your practice by starting in different postures and with the whip curled up in your hand or on your belt.

The skill to **disarm** and trip with the whip is very straightforward. To strip a weapon from an attacker simply allow the whip to uncurl until about a foot of the end wraps around the item. Once wrapped and taut, it is only necessary to grip with two hands and tug sharply.

To acquire this skill, balance a broom at shoulder height horizontally some distance away and practice wrapping and tugging until adept.

To trip an opponent is a difficult skill to master but only requires practice to complete.

Wrap the end of the weapon around one or two ankles of your adversary and tug once taught. The wisdom required here is that you must attempt the wrap from an angle of forty-five degrees to your adversary. Attempting to wrap straightforward just results in tangling and losing your weapon.

The technique to carry out close quarter blocking is to grip the handle and the curled whip forming a square to receive the strike. This is also true of the Ball and Chain.

Block and hook around the back of the neck of your adversary.

Use the weapon handle just like a stick.

Pull your adversary down onto your rising knee to impact on the face.

To make the impact focused you must point your foot toes down so that bone and not muscle connect first.

CHAPTER IV:
WEAPONS SKILLS

Knife Throwing

In Part Three of the Syllabus the fighter is introduced to throwing the knife by the blade or the hilt. It must first be realised that the knife is **NEVER THROWN AWAY** in a combat situation unless to preserve life and then only if the balance of odds is such that you feel you can down an attacker with it.

It follows then that in English Combat the knife is thrown primarily by the hilt as it presumes you are fighting with it at the time and to change it around to throw by the blade is an unnecessary waste of time.

This all means that if you will throw it at all then it must work. You must down the attacker with the first penetration.

The physical ability to throw a knife depends again on practice, practice and more practice. It is extremely simple in theory. I myself have erected a target board in my garden and practice several times a week. I usually do it as soon as I arrive home to loosen up my arms, as it is a good exercise as well as being a necessary skill. All fighters must be fully aware that if you are going to use a knife in a fight you will get cut, the same if you are involved in a an exchange of punches you will be punched. What we will learn to do is minimize all the risks and actually take the upper hand. The type of knife that you throw is of no account as all can be thrown. More important is consistency with the way it is done. What you will learn here is the principle to apply.

I throw all my weapons in the same way and usually hit my target with nine out of ten throws at playing card size from standing, kneeling, lying or moving, from ten feet and from twenty feet. I do this outside as it is more likely to be needed out than in. Outside throwing means you have to contend with the weather also. It is not the same throwing across a centrally heated living room as it is throwing outside on a blustery day pouring with rain. Train outside to throw and inside becomes child's play.

When throwing blades of any shape it is necessary only to practice often to develop skill. Some people have an inbuilt instinct for balance, distance and accuracy. It is still possible however, to be able to be very good without this instinct through perseverance.

It is advisable to learn basic first aid when using blades in case of accidental injury. All blades cut and some cuts get infected extremely quickly. Learn in particular how to stem the flow of blood.

As a general rule, elevate the wound, if it still bleeds, use direct pressure with the fingers then if not stopped, direct pressure with a pad (up to three max) to absorb the blood. If still it bleeds, apply indirect pressure to the Brachial or Femoral pulse points. Do this no longer than ten minutes. In all cases seek medical advice.

> **TERRY GLOVER'S TRAINING TIPS**
>
> Use a knife you are happy with regularly for accuracy, then use many different types to develop ability.

CHAPTER IV: WEAPONS SKILLS

The following illustrations show how to throw the knife by blade and hilt.

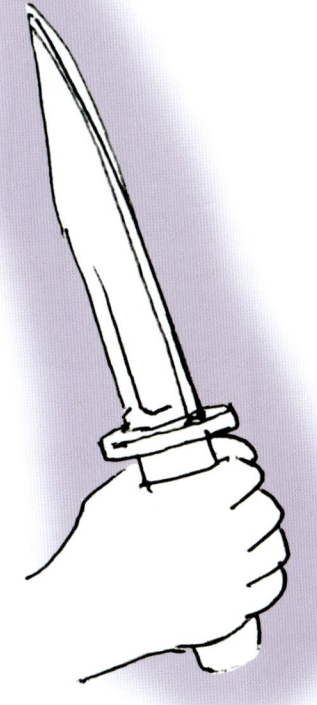

When throwing by the hilt you must hold the knife as if you mean to stab. Have a strong grip.

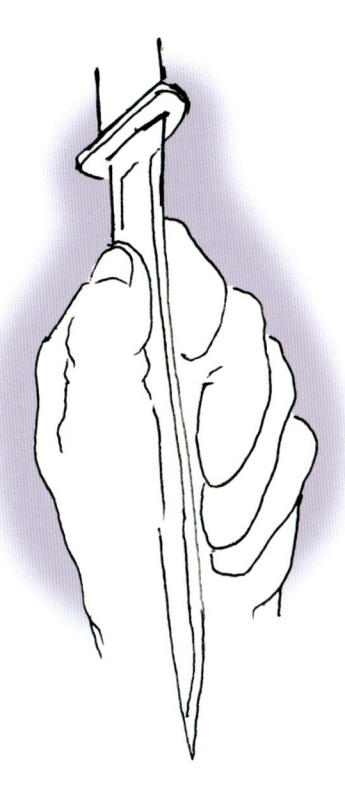

When throwing by the blade, hold the knife along the flat side and not the sharp or blunt edge.

How ever you decide to throw, you then hold out your free hand to sight along, and throw with a hard thrust to penetrate well.

If you stand six and one half paces away from a target and throw a few times you will start to develop a feel for the flight and effort needed to affect a stick.

Throw with legs slightly bent and relaxed. Throw straight at the target and follow through with the throwing arm.

Never throw *to* a target throw *through* a target

After developing skill at six and one half paces, double the distance and find your new mark and practice again. Repeat this until you achieve hitting a man-sized target centrally from at least thirty feet. Then come back to six and one half paces and start again, this time trying for accuracy.

CHAPTER IV: WEAPONS SKILLS

Throwing the Axe

Throwing the axe would seem to be a limited skill for contemporary street situations but it is increasingly common to find axes and hatchets used in street brawls and attacks. The machete and hatchet are fairly commonplace with gangs.

A well-thrown axe or hatchet, will penetrate bone with hardly any effort and care must be taken to throw using common sense and not around children and animals. The process is illustrated below:

> Throwing the axe is similar to throwing the knife and requires the same focus and release by following through with the hand. This means that the hand motion keeps going towards the target instead of dropping down straight away.

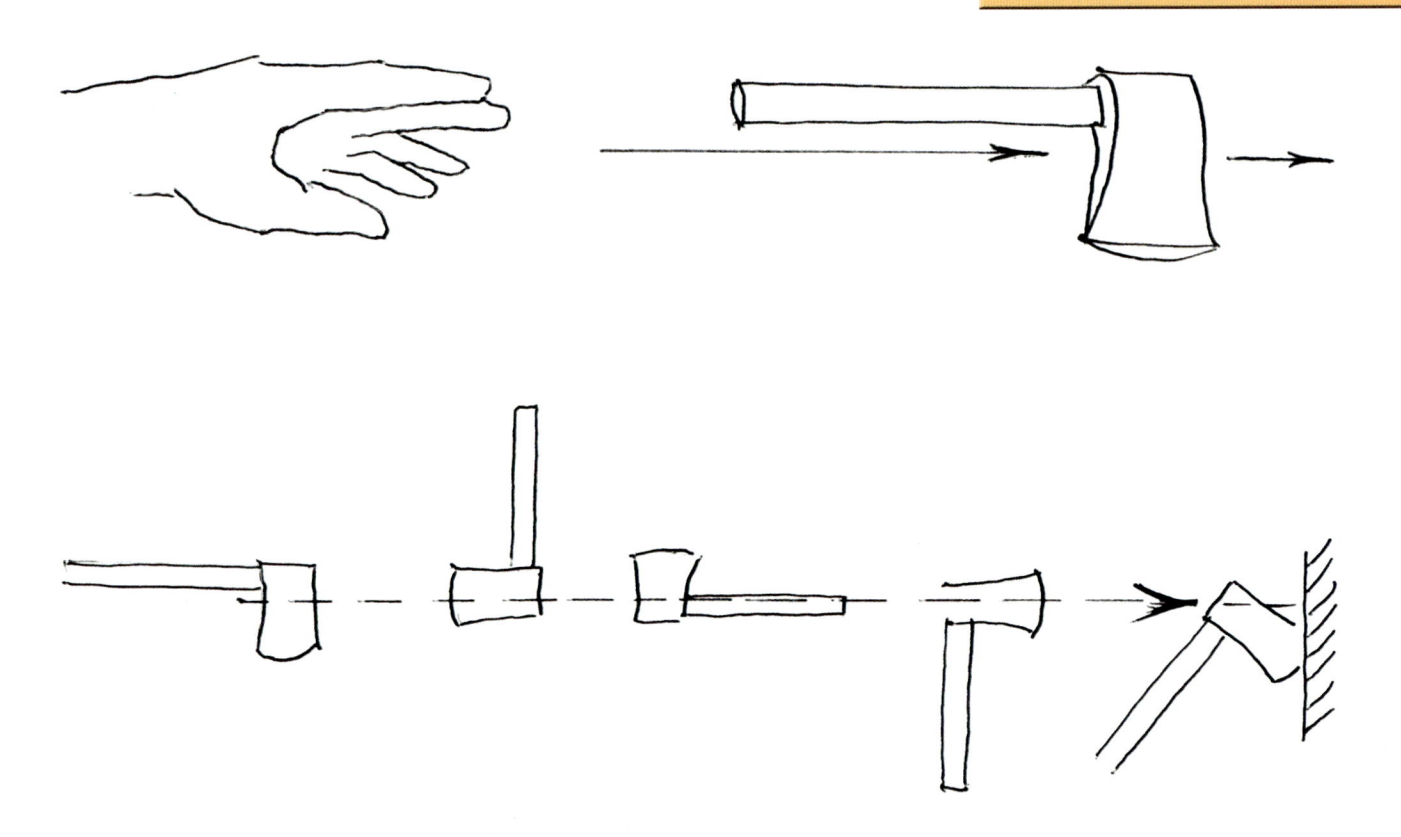

When the axe is in flight the head will tumble and turn the handle around itself. The thrower only needs to judge the moment of impact by starting at six and one half paces from a target and practicing to obtain the optimum point of release for the set distance.

Do start off with the axe held vertical, blade facing the target.

Once six and one half paces are easy to stick, try again at twenty-two and forty paces.

The Quarterstaff Throw

The Quarterstaff throw is simply done hefted by the balance centre and must land point first without tumbling. Pretend it is a Spear. Aim at a target and practice often.

CHAPTER IV: WEAPONS SKILLS

Quarterstaff Disarms

The disarming techniques for the Quarterstaff are illustrated below:

Practice disarming the Quarterstaff slowly many times and then try it quickly.

Once you have acquired a good level of skill, try to disarm in a fight situation.

Start with block and counter, suddenly drop your own Quarterstaff, and then take away the weapon belonging to your opponent. Hit him with it to provide a lesson.

Once you can do this then progress to facing an adversary charging towards you at high speed, now take his weapon away.

Glover Family English Combat Fighting System

TERRY GLOVER'S TRAINING TIPS

When training with blades remember that the closer you are to your opponent, the safer you are.

Notice here that the same basic moves are applied in disarming a large axe that were also used to disarm a Quarterstaff.

When practising this sequence, be aware that leaning forward and suddenly turning after striking at the face with the elbow allows for swift efficient disarms by making your opponent disorientated.

Always practice safely when using blades of any size.

Make sure you know and can apply simple first aid for cuts and amputations.

CHAPTER IV: WEAPONS SKILLS

Stick Disarms

The following photos illustrate the moves needed to disarm a stick. When practicing these moves do them slowly at first and as a drill, followed by doing them in the middle of a block and counter session.

When you are proficient at them, try letting your training partner attempt to cave in your skull, before he does, disarm him. If you do it, you are now competent.

Disarm One:

Press with the lower part of the stick on the forearm to affect the disarm.

Practice at speed. Practice slowly, and then repeat.

Now do the same at home and in the street.

CHAPTER IV:
WEAPONS SKILLS

Disarm Two:

Disarm number two is easily done after practice and gives the first glimmer of the possibility to disarm an opponent using only two angles.

If one becomes adept at all these following angle disarms, try eliminating them all and using number one and two to disarm from any angle.

If you can do this then forget the others as you have instinctive abilities and do not need them. If you cannot do this, then keep practising: one day it will come to you.

Disarm Three:

Block and drop the elbow in one rapid movement:

Push forward to affect the release. Use skill, not strength:

Turn your body to the right and step back with the right foot:

Disarm Four (same as two but lower):

Left hand upside down when blocking, then pivot right and utilise technique to disarm - not strength:

Disarm Five:

For street use, strike with the butt on the hand to affect the disarm.

84

**CHAPTER IV:
WEAPONS SKILLS**

Disarm Six:

Snap the left hand back and right hand forward simultaneously, pushing your cudgel sharply.

Disarm Seven:

Drop your body weight suddenly as you block. Execute the block and elbow drop in one rapid movement:

Disarm Eight:

Live hand (left) upside down for the block.

Grasp the attacker's thumb pad with your fingers, pushing your thumb against the knuckle row to open the grip.

(continued on following page)

86

**CHAPTER IV:
WEAPONS SKILLS**

Disarm Nine:

Disarm Ten:

At this point in learning the way of disarming it is necessary to realise that body angling and changing direction are important. In Disarm Ten, for example, it can be seen that to affect the technique the fighter must angle first to the right, left and then right again.

The last two of the twelve show the need to move up and down, then backwards and forward. Constant motion, with many changes of angles, in a fast relaxed manner, makes a good fighter.

**CHAPTER IV:
WEAPONS SKILLS**

Disarm Eleven:

Twist your left hand grip to affect the release.

Disarm Twelve:

Photos 5 and 6 above show a counter strike to angle No 1.

90

**CHAPTER IV:
WEAPONS SKILLS**

These disarms are easy to carry out in a training hall but take long hours of practice to perfect, so…

PRACTICE!   PRACTICE!   PRACTICE!

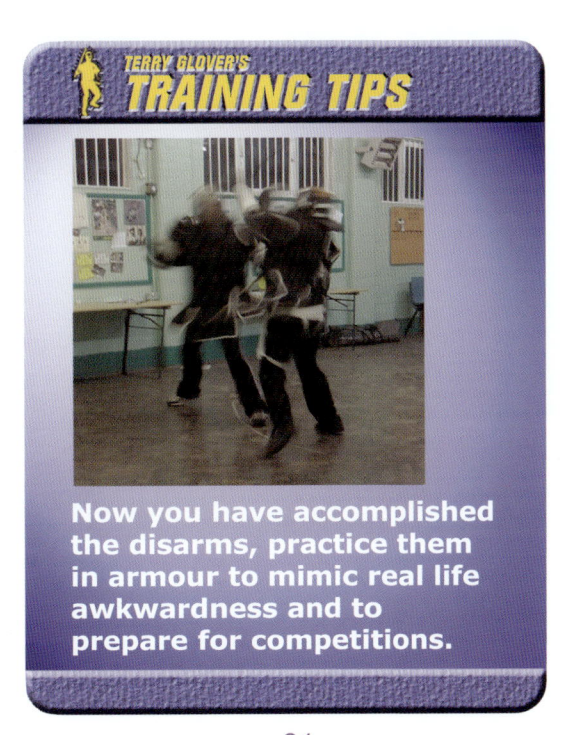

TERRY GLOVER'S TRAINING TIPS

Now you have accomplished the disarms, practice them in armour to mimic real life awkwardness and to prepare for competitions.

CHAPTER IV:
WEAPONS SKILLS

In the following sequence we see how the whip is defensively held curled up in the hand until needed to strike at full length. Sometimes there is no room and so it can be utilised at close quarters still curled:

The next sequence shows another option at close quarters:

CHAPTER V:
ADVANCED WEAPON SKILLS

It is interesting to note that an assailant can be brought down from either side once the whip is around his neck. Here we see the take down affected from the left side.

Practice with both sides until skill is acquired. Then do it in a combat scenario.

In English Combat it is useful to notice that most people being right handed will adopt an orthodox stance when facing you (left foot forward). As long as you keep practicing adopting the unorthodox stance you will compel your opponent to advance towards you with at least one step to land a strike, which will give you a short but very important advantage, as you will have prior warning of the attack.

Face your training partner in the positions seen in the accompanying photograph and ask him to attack you. He will keep warning you of his intention as soon as he moves allowing you to effect the counter block or strike.

Any weapon you hold must be held slightly forward of your leading right leg. This will cause the opponent to be aware of it and he will judge his distance and timing by it. If you then quickly move it just prior to receiving an attack it will cause the attacker to be incorrect in his judgement and timing.

This stance also allows you to bring your rear foot forward as he steps forward so that you can affect a foot sweep without making it obvious.

95

CHAPTER V:
ADVANCED WEAPON SKILLS

The foot move can also be changed mid flow to become a jamming move simply by turning the foot sideways so that his advancing foot stumbles into it.

It is also useful to know that if you line up your front foot with his front foot it will be almost impossible for him to kick you with his back leg without warning. Throughout the combat, continue to look at the top of his chest for good peripheral vision.

The Ball and Chain

The Ball and Chain is astonishingly fast and can attack from ludicrous angles seemingly defying logic.

The basic moves with this weapon are the same as the Single Stick and Quarter Staff.

In Medieval England this weapon was favoured in its single ball form by Men at Arms and in it's double ball form by members of the clergy, travelling Friars dubbing it the 'Holy Sprinkler'.

All the strikes are carried out using the English Broadsword Circle angles. The additional possibilities are outlined below:

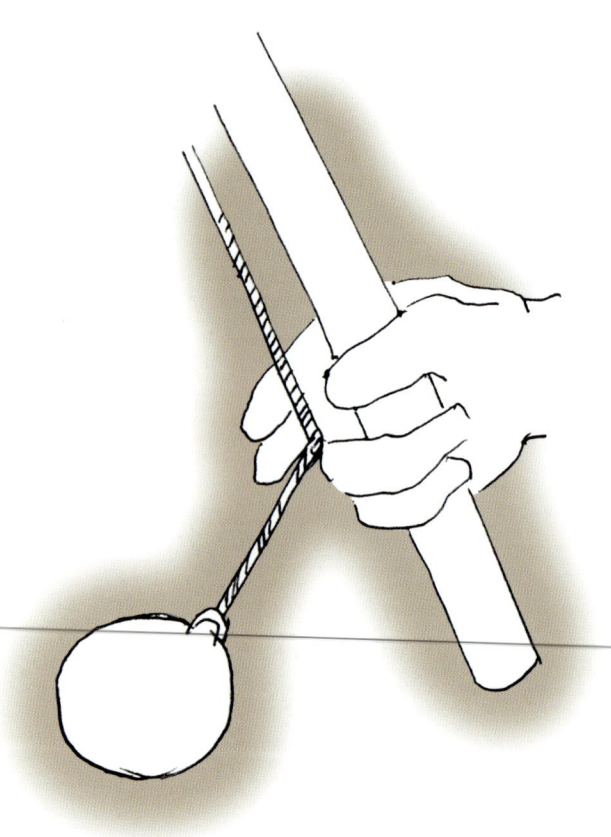

When using the Ball and Chain it should primarily be used like a Single Stick and the ball and chain should be deftly kept out of the fray by the index and middle finger.

The strike with the ball is done suddenly and sparingly. Swinging the ball around threateningly does not help to defeat an opponent. Rather it will cause him to guffaw at a weapon out of control.

Glover Family English Combat Fighting System

The weapon can be used by holding onto the ball and striking with the shaft, much to the surprise of an opponent who believes that if you have a Ball and Chain you must use the Ball to strike.

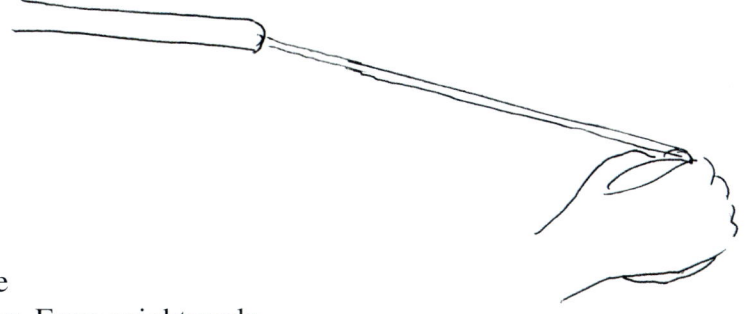

To block with this weapon of surprise, hold the the ball above the point where the chain attaches. Form a right angle to block a strike coming from the top or left in the illustrated case. Bear in mind that the block can be used on the other side simply by lowering the right arm and holding the ball up so that the chain is now across the top of the head thus blocking equally to the right and above simultaneously.

> The way to appreciate this weapon is to fight with it and enjoy it. It will continuously surprise you and your opponent. Practice often and with alacrity. It is exhilarating.

Attack blocked from above

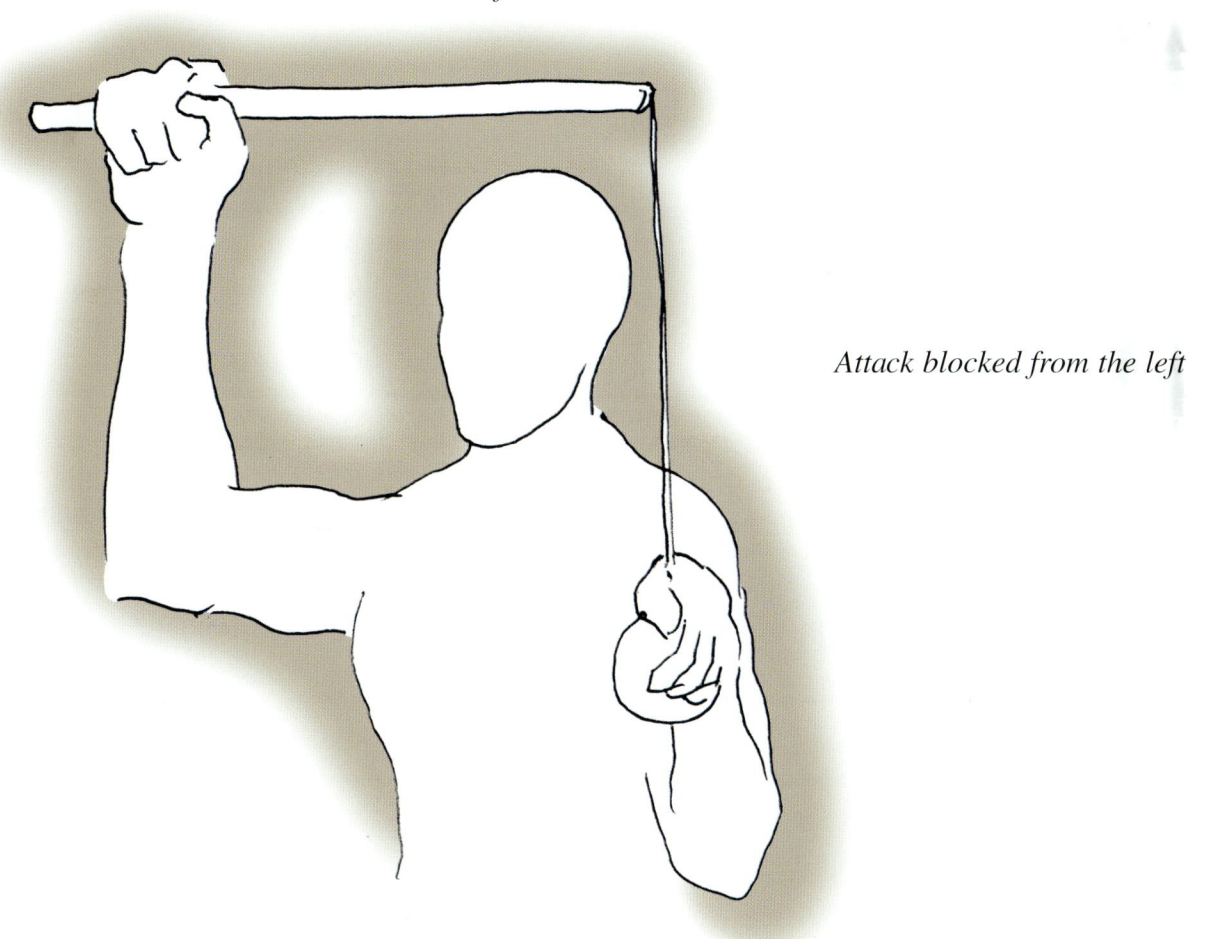

Attack blocked from the left

97

**CHAPTER V:
ADVANCED WEAPON SKILLS**

As soon as the attacking weapon or fist is blocked the Ball and Chain should be moved to strike in counter attack with the utmost speed. Moving the weapon like a Single Stick will ensure that the strikes are fast and accurate.

Make sure that when you strike, you strike through the target without hesitation, as any faltering will allow the ball to rebound to hit you instead of continuing along its intended path.

Practice this effect on a hanging bag and you will understand how it happens. Strike the bag and imagine that it does not exist as you strike through it instead of dropping the ball on the surface. You will witness the ball seeming to continue through it as if by magic.

Now strike the bag and let the ball bounce on the surface and be prepared to cry out when the ball hits you.

Knife

The knife is already covered in this training manual to accommodate the syllabus.

Once the syllabus is completed it is now time to increase your skill and knowledge with this private sidearm.

In open conflict it is always advisable to use the knife in conjunction with other weapons. You can use a Single Stick and knife, a Rapier and knife, and Broadsword and knife etc.

When forced to use the knife on it's own it is necessary to know one very peculiar fact. If you are armed with a knife you are at a disadvantage to an unarmed knife fighter.

To illustrate this point, take a knife and attempt to hold onto it and at the same time, strangle your training partner.

You have now learned that to use a knife on it's own can be tricky. You are immediately denied some fighting skills.

In general, you must attempt to utilise the knife in much the same way as the Single Stick. Doing this will allow you to realise you have now gained potential with all blades, be they the machete, sword or kitchen knife.

Disarming someone holding a knife is not too difficult but takes a lot of practice to acquire the skill. Look back at Chapter II, including knife stripping.

Let us look at an aspect of the knife that is not given due consideration, that is to say the way and time the knife can be thrown. Here is a photograph of some knives that are successful throwers. Notice that they all have something in common: no guard.

Although all of the knives in the photograph can by thrown successfully and accurately by a practised thrower, any one using them in close combat would find fingers being sliced off and wrists cut and bleeding followed by dropping your weapon. The reason is that a guard is in place normally to protect against these things.

I have spent many happy years throwing knives of all kinds to see which suit me best. I have fallen in love with a knife that suits me perfectly. This knife is a British Army Jungle Survival Knife, which has a multitude of uses, but one for which I believe it is born for is throwing.

Straight away you need to see what this weapon looks like so here is an illustration:

It has size and weight and good balance. It can be thrown equally by the blade or by the hilt. It is heavy enough to go over a guard or defence, and heavy enough to penetrate deeply. It is strong, and over twenty years in the military that I have used it there is not one occasion where it has broken.

This knife also can be used at close quarters as it has a generous hilt built in.

CHAPTER V:
ADVANCED WEAPON SKILLS

The only proviso to an amateur attempting to use it is that the hilt has a piece jutting out at the base, which is ostensibly to maintain a grip, but gets in the way when throwing. I have shaved off this piece on mine.

When **throwing a knife** it is worth repeating the advice from previous chapters, and that is if you have to throw this weapon at all it must be because you are certain of hitting and stopping your target, and not for show.

If you throw away your knife in a street situation and others are armed, you are losing immediately.

When throwing a knife you must do so in as simple a way as possible to start with.

In English Combat I teach always to throw by holding the hilt of the weapon as you can do so immediately without turning it around.

If you throw by the blade you have turned it and this took time. In this time period you could be struck down.

Find yourself a space outside to begin with and check for livestock or human presence. Never throw in practice with onlookers if possible. Knives can come back at you from a target faster than you can throw them sometimes.

Set up a target about six and one half paces and about chest height. The target to be human body width and made of soft wood at first. The thickness should be as close to a foot deep as possible. (This means you can also use it to throw axes.)

The best targets are easily made from cut up tree trunks, with the bottom or top as the sticking surface.

TERRY GLOVER'S TRAINING TIPS

When throwing knives and axes, walk towards, past and away from a target and then spin and throw suddenly to reflect real life.

Throw by holding the hilt and raising it to shoulder height so that the knife blade point is aiming at the sky. Point your free hand at the target as an aiming sight and throw by hurling forward and keep your throwing hand going out so that you have followed through. Leave your throwing hand pointing as if willing the knife to the correct place to stick. When the knife sticks, lower the throwing hand.

You will find that the knife probably just bounced off the target and it was disappointing to see. Don't worry; this is just the start of a long love/hate relationship with a blade. At first you will be really frustrated, but then after a few throws one will stick and the feeling of pleasure gained will be almost euphoric.

What is more important is that each stick will force into your neuromuscular system the correct balance, speed and hold of the knife. Each time you throw from then on will reinforce the correct sequence on your body mechanics. From here on in it will just be a case of practice, practice and practice.

As time passes and sticking from this distance to such a large target will be so easy as to lose its challenge appeal. You can then start moving back another six paces and starting again.

Aim at first for only one turn of the knife, then proceed to one and a half and then two or more.

Try to finish your knife throwing practice session with a go at sticking on a playing card size target from about twenty feet. Then go back to your successful distance and stick some in as a last throw. This will finish on a good note.

Good luck, and all it takes to become good is plenty of practice.

When I am asked if a thrown knife can really put down an angry charging man I tell of a man called Tony Cascarella, who on March 16, 1976 in Florida, killed a charging wild boar with thrown Bowie Axe knives, the first penetrating the skull of the 275 pound monster between the eyes cleaving into the skull to separate the brain. This was a charging beast at twenty feet. The fearsome animal stopped and spun in a dance of death whereby Tony loosed two more knives to speed the kill, dropping it cold.

It is a rare man that can charge as fearsomely and as gamely as a wild boar intent on slicing you to mincemeat, which it is capable of doing within seconds.

A thrown knife is dangerous and a knife thrown by a practiced thrower is deadly.

In Medieval Europe, including England, there has always existed skills to deal with weapons.

This is an illustration of unarmed grappling with an armed attacker.

This is amply covered in Medieval grappling taken from the Flos Duelletorum of Dei Liberi (1410), Hans Talhoffer's Fectbuch (1459) ("Fight Book") and others.

Marozzo's Opera Nova (1536) incorporates knife fighting and unarmed versus knife.

Once having learned from this training manual all that you can, it is tempting to progress to other manuals and books, and try to learn more and more.

In England there is an expression,

Don't be a Jack-of-all-trades and master of none.

This tells us that learning a little and mastering it is preferable and more productive than learning ten thousand skills and mastering none. Pick which you like and become a master. Look at the others out of interest.

The Axe

The axe used within the English Combat System is principally a light hand axe with a wooden handle. The wooden handle allows for extended versatile use without degradation unlike the metal handled variety which only seem to last a couple of days after hard use.

Photographed here are my own axes used in axe drills and for throwing. I have used these in training halls and outside for throwing for years in all weathers without problems.

The axes on the left have a one and a quarter pound head and straight wooden handle. The axes on the right have a one-pound head and curved grip handle. Each has its own characteristics.

Fundamentally you should choose a set of axes for training or throwing by the way they feel to you. It is like a comfortable pair of shoes. Heft the weapon and if it feels right in your hand then it will perform well for you. Usually about a pound to a pound and a half axe head weight is about right. Anything more and it becomes unwieldy.

Use the same targetry as the knife and increase the throwing distance by one and a half paces but carry out the same process of training.

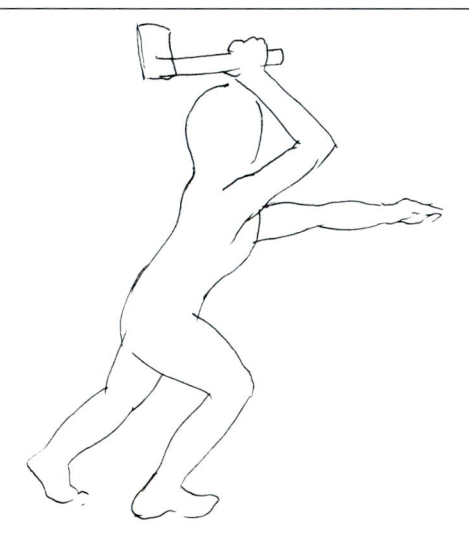

In preparing to throw it must be understood that successful axe throwing comes from control of the axe before and during the flight. It must be thrown strongly and with conviction.

Follow through with the throwing hand. Aim with the free hand. Move into the throw with the body from a balanced relaxed stance.

Keep the rear heel up like a sprinter.

To throw backwards, practice from this illustrated stance. At first it seems odd and impractical until you stick the axe into the target and then you will realise it is superb.

It is also much faster than turning around.

To throw horizontally is extremely difficult as a skill to master, and needs plenty of practice.

Persevere, and then demonstrate to someone - they will believe you are accomplishing the impossible.

It is necessary to understand that the axe a has different blocking approach than the other weapons you have so far learned.

103

CHAPTER V:
ADVANCED WEAPON SKILLS

When attacked you can use the ability of this weapon to hook and thrust at close quarters.

This sequence of blocking and countering with a thrust is illustrated for your convenience.

Take note that the free hand plays an important part in capturing the attackers arm.

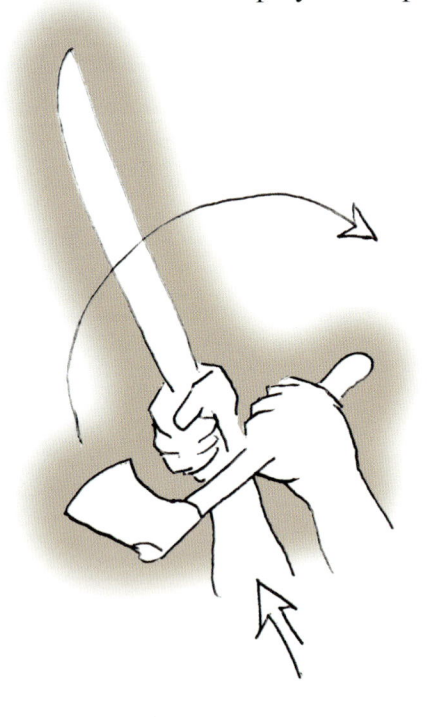

Receive the blow on the front of the axe shaft so that the shaft and head form a V-shape in case of slippage.

In a continuing motion execute a circle to the right and press down with the axe.

Complete the circular move and then suddenly and violently thrust the axe head upwards to smash into the attacker's face.

Once impact has been made, the axe can be brought down quickly to sever the hand holding the weapon.

The process on receiving a blow from the right is to block, capture the arm, thrust into the face and slice off the hand with the weapon without needing to carry out the circular snaring move.

104

**CHAPTER V:
ADVANCED WEAPON SKILLS**

The Quarter Staff

The Quarter Staff has already been amply illustrated and described in preceding chapters apart from one important aspect.

> **Fluidity**
>
> To achieve fluidity it is necessary to be unencumbered and learn to move the grip to a pertinent point from which to execute a block or blow.

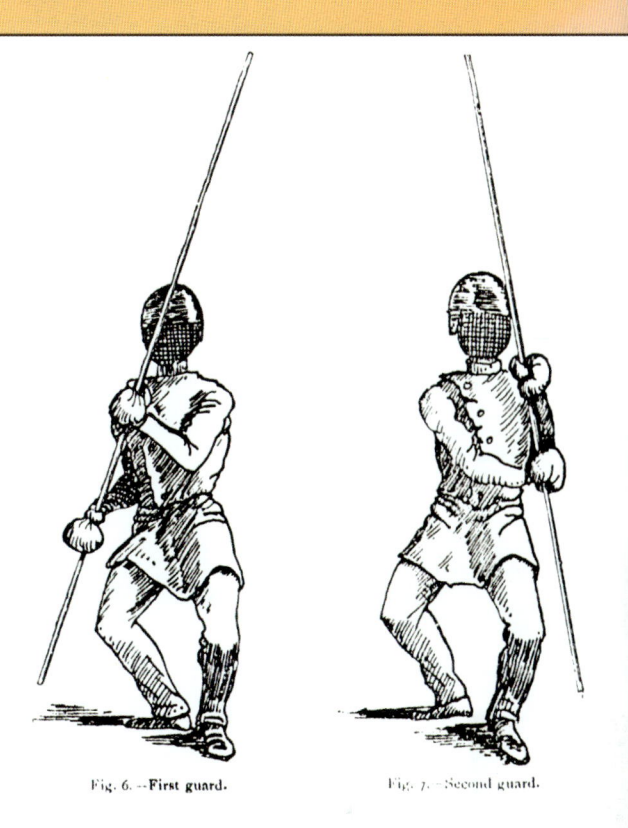

The two adversaries in this illustration are dressed to protect themselves but also to be able to nimbly move about the fighting area.

As we develop materials in this modern age it is worth considering clothing and protection from past ages if it works for you.

Practice developing your fighting skills, with the Quarter Staff, while dressed in different attire.

To achieve fluidity it is only necessary to either slide the gripping hands on the Quarter Staff or to let go entirely with one hand.

I enjoy fighting with two Quarter Staff, one in each hand. Try to use the weapon in one hand only during sparring matches and you will learn quickly to use the sliding hand deftly as you find some blocks need two hands to execute.

Fig. 6.—First guard.   Fig. 7.—Second guard.

Another way to accomplish the sliding skill is to imagine the weapon is a two handed sword and fight accordingly.

Don't miss out **sweeping moves** with the weapon during sparring.

When sweeping an opponent, place the weapon vigorously behind the ankle or knee and slide the relevant part of his anatomy sideways. Capitalise on this misfortune with a hefty impact to his skull. Now the only thing left to do is,

PRACTICE!   PRACTICE!   PRACTICE!

CHAPTER V:
ADVANCED WEAPON SKILLS

Single stick fight action from the 8th World Eskrima Kali Arnis World Championships 2004, Cebu, Philippines

English Combat Honours at the 2004 World Championships:
Abby Steady - Female Single Stick World Champion
Sam Martin Jnr - Male Junior Single Stick World Champion

CHAPTER VI:
SPECIAL SKILLS

Doorway Practice

It is true to say, that once a person has trained until competent in the training hall, it is necessary to train in ones home and surrounding area also.

The techniques learned in the English Combat system will stand you in good stead against the street ruffian or interloper found at night in your home, however, the fighter must adjust the approach to accommodate irregularities found in these areas.

Start your home and family environment practice with the doorway. The doorway poses some tricky problems to overcome. It is not possible to carry out wild or full swings either armed or unarmed here. One must train with another fighter pretending to be the antagonist.

Try standing right side on in the doorway and with any weapon in your right hand. This allows you to bring it to bear quickly. Use the front foot to kick, foot sweep or jam a technique and stand just outside the doorway if against one antagonist or just inside if there are too many to overcome quickly, as this reduces them to one at a time for you to deal with.

The prime attacking weapons when unarmed are the straight right and left cross punches coupled with elbow strikes from any angle. The elbow strikes allow one to close in and bring down the antagonist effectively. Practice this often.

The prime attacking weapons when armed are the stick and knife as close quarter specialist items. Try using them separately against your practice antagonist, then in combination.

Consider lowering the height of your doorway. For example, I am only five foot seven inches in height, so is my doorway. I fit and can fight perfectly inside all my doorways.

Stairway Practice

It is interesting to note that when castles sprang up around England after the Norman invasion, they were designed with purpose to be defended from attackers inside, as well as out. To this end you will find that on inspection, if visiting a castle, one discovers that a person being pressed backwards up a stairway is more in control than one doing the pressing.

Consider a spiral stairway, the defender can strike easily with a sword in the right hand due to built in space on his right. This is not so in the attacker's case who finds his right-hand space diminished considerably by the inner spiral.

Consider next the long stairway. Usually there are flat platforms every so often, which now we refer to as landings. The platforms allow the defender to manoeuvre adroitly to counter the slow moving attacker, forced to advance up steps with diminished manoeuvrability.

This is known as controlling the high ground, something that all military personnel will understand as a basic requirement to domination of a battlefield.

I have never believed, by the way, in the modern approach to home protection. These unfortunate times seem to require a panic room in which to hide for personal protection. Why indeed must one look at it this way? Why not cause the interloper to panic with fear or terror instead? Much more fun!

Make your family home a no-go area to these ruffians.

Another approach is to position items like metal pens or propelling pencils as decoration along the walls of stairways. These innocuous looking items are dealers of immense pain at close quarters and are simple to use. All that one has to do is to hold one with a portion extending a couple of inches out of the clenched fist either side and you have the ability to punch or puncture flesh or bone as you wish.

Dealing With Gang Attacks

Dealing with gang attacks is fraught with danger and not to be considered at all if you can sensibly avoid it. However, if you find yourself in this scenario remember this always please:

Gangs act like a pack of wild animals. When their blood is up, you are limited in possible responses as they react to any sudden movement or display of vulnerability.

One approach much advocated is to do as you are told or beg and plead for your life, or possessions. Do this at your peril. If you do as you are told the gang will take liberties with you as well as your possessions. Why give them an easy ride?

Don't take on gangs if you can avoid them. Although they are just bullies, they are dangerous. The danger comes from sheer weight of numbers. Run away and if you cannot run, sell your soul as dearly and as violently as you can. Pick one of them and take that one down with you, eat that person, clamp your teeth into their throat and don't let go, scratch and pull off ears, gouge out eyes, give no quarter, as they deserve none.

To call gang members animals is in fact a bad thing to do, as it is an insult to animals.

Techniques that are helpful to a Lady

As a lady going about your normal daily business it is nice to be complimented and treated well, but this does not always happen.

Presence of mind and good health are watchwords in the survival of a woman.

When a woman is attacked it is normally quick and from the rear, catching her by surprise. Most attacks therefore go to ground almost immediately.

It is better to avoid an attack than to try and deal with it when it does. To this end, read on.

Most attacks occur when one is alone, in the dark, or in quiet places. This obviously need to be addressed. If you suspect potential risk, consider the following in depth:

- Never habitually take the same route every day if you can avoid it.

- Avoid short cuts through car parks, alleys, woods or dark deserted places.

- Avoid being on your own on foot if possible.

- Remember that most attacks on females take place only a short distance from home so take care on arriving just as you do when setting off.

- Have your house keys in your hand. They enable you to enter your home quickly and provide a weapon at the same time.

- Avoid walking down the street with a mobile phone to your ear. Leave a call until you are with someone or at home or work.

- If you are attacked and not held, then scream, bite, scratch and kick your way past or away and run. Go to the nearest obvious habitation, any lighted buildings. If you cannot open a building door and the light is on, smash the windows and keep screaming. The occupant cannot pretend you are not there after that.

- Scream violently at your attacker, yell foul words and behave demented. (If your attacker harbours sexual plans, he will decide otherwise very quickly if he believes he will be savagely torn and bitten).

- Use daily objects as weapons. The law does not allow a person to carry offensive weapons. A rolled up magazine or metal cased pen are just a couple of items to turn into offensive weapons in a moment (I provide a list of such items for you to peruse and select.) Perhaps even pick something different with each outfit?

Such rules banning offensive weapons are actually good sense, as a weapon recognised by an attacker can get into their hands and be used against you. Unrecognisable weapons are good sense. Get to know them.

When in the street, a lady should be careful of someone that seems to be following them. If you believe this to be true, here is a way to find out.

Cross the street opposite a large shop or house window and look into the reflection as you do so. This will enable you to see if the person follows you. Now cross back in a similar fashion, the stalker will expose themselves if they follow.

Should you be followed, go up to someone and ask for help. If there is no one about,… what are you doing there?

Get to know and practice the English Combat system, this will enable you to fight back. Be fast, be vicious, run away screaming.

In particular become well versed in releases from grabs – see Chapter III. Here are some additional techniques for use if you are taken down.

The 'scissors' and how to lie down:

Reposition yourself to be able to jump in quickly.

111

CHAPTER VI:
SPECIAL SKILLS

The side-foot trip:

Push up with your foot as well as pushing away.

Heel kick to knee followed by scissors and heel stomp:

112

CHAPTER VI:
SPECIAL SKILLS

Maintain a guard in case you fail to topple the attacker.

Heel grab and double heel strike to abdomen:

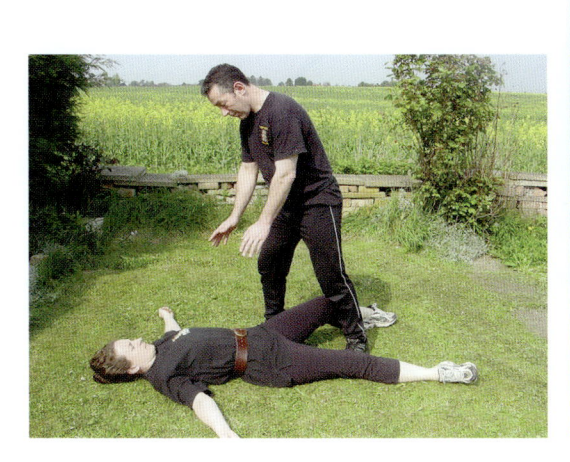

Don't let the attacker rest their bodyweight on you – strike and grasp quickly.

113

CHAPTER VI:
SPECIAL SKILLS

Dealing with Bullies at School

Dealing with bullies at school can be a very daunting task for a child. It is a simple case of fighting back and defeating the bullies. However, it is easy to say and seemingly impossible to do.

First it is necessary to give a child confidence. Acquiring skills and some success in open fighting competition best does this. This will show the child that it is possible to win a situation even if the odds are not on your side.

Let your child know that saying **NO** is a viable option because they can enforce it if necessary.

With this knowledge the child can progress.

Once again, this is easy to say and not so easy to do. All children should be encouraged to see that they can defend themselves. Just because a child has learned to fight does not make that child a thug or bully. Rather it helps give confidence to say no.

It is circumstances and environmental pressures, usually from contemporary peers, which become the instigator. Some children have no interest in fighting at all, even to defend themselves. These children would benefit from early attendance at training sessions before they have the ability to say no to their parents.

Ask the school to set up English Combat classes in the evenings for family groups so that the parents get to train and know the children involved and their parents. This can allow all present to see that no one is a threat and mixing is possible.

If training in any shape or form at any age seems impossible for any reason, it is not always a good thing for a parent to go to the bullies with threats simply because as soon as they leave, the unfortunate child then gets extra bullying which causes them to resent their own parents' intrusion.

The next option is to attend the school and go to the Head Teacher and say what is happening. See if the school has a policy to stop it happening. Stop your child from taking mobile phones and money to school as this leads to theft and bullying. Let them wear what is popular but never buy the most expensive, as this becomes a target for more theft and bullying.

CHAPTER VI:
SPECIAL SKILLS

Finally, the parents can attend English Combat classes themselves in their neighbourhood and gain a reputation which causes other parents to stop their children bullying for fear of consequential action from you.

**If you know of anyone being bullied
then buy them a copy of this book.**

Dealing with Bullies at Work

Bullies at work usually come into two categories, the boss or the idiot.

If it is your boss who is bullying you it is wise to consider this, if you let it happen it will probably get worse and almost never better.

In order to deal with bullying at work you can try the straightforward approach and just say you feel you are being bullied. If this only causes merriment from the boss and even more bullying, then remind your boss that you can go to a Solicitor for legal representation and will do so if it doesn't stop.

If the bullying does not stop then simply leave. Better to be temporarily out of work with your self-respect and dignity intact, then to loathe yourself.

Another alternative is to train well in English Combat and since you will leave anyway, you can try to reason with the clown in a quiet corridor with no witnesses. What will you have to lose… your job?

Do yourself a favour and keep your self-respect.

If it is just an idiot at work, simply go straight to the quiet corridor option. The bullying will stop if you stop being a willing victim.

Training in English Combat allows one to stop worrying about these people anyway, since they will not be capable of carrying out their threats.

If you know of anyone being bullied then buy them a copy of this book.

Daily objects as weapons

Here are some examples of everyday objects as weapons. Incorporating principles and techniques found in the English Combat Fighting System you can use all of these improvised weapons.

Magazines

Strike also as if with the butt of a cudgel for speed, as shown below:

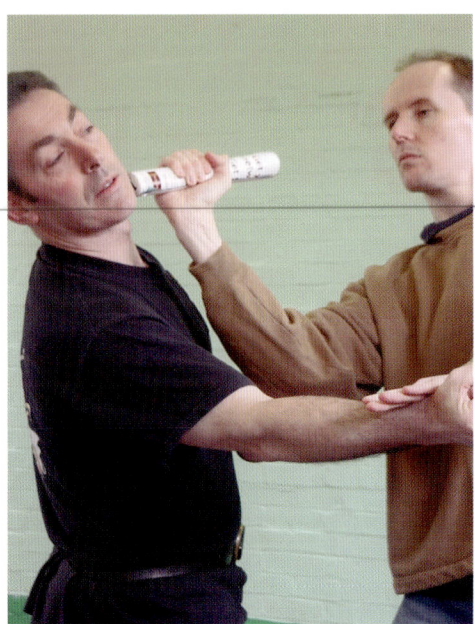

116

CHAPTER VI:
SPECIAL SKILLS

Coins

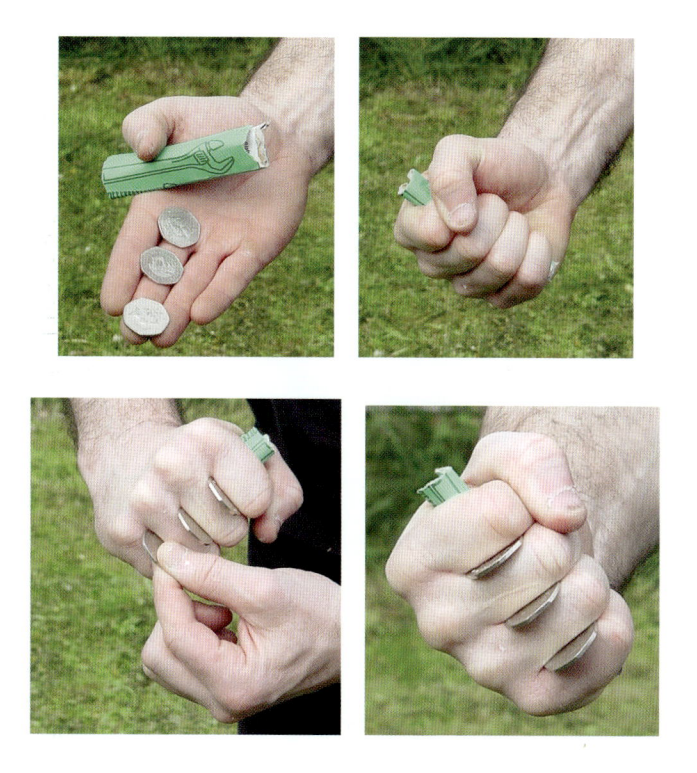

Tuck the coins in tightly.

Pens

Metal cased puncture weapon.

Strike to soft sensitive areas for maximum pain to release the hold.

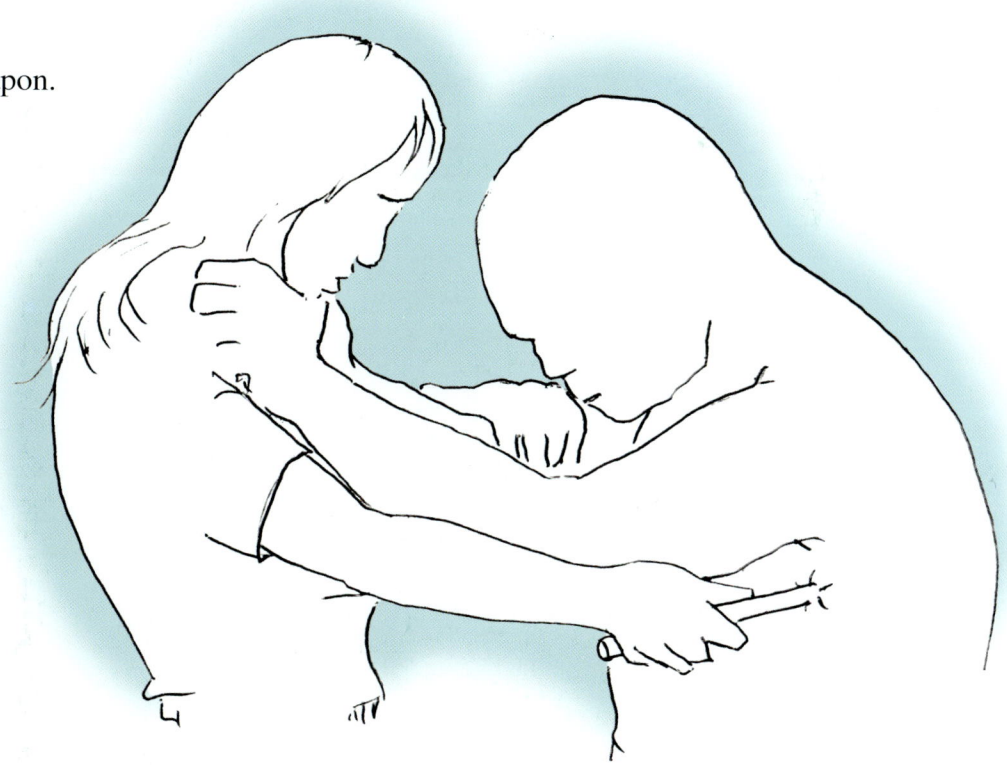

CHAPTER VI:
SPECIAL SKILLS

Umbrella

Front kick disguised, belly poked, foot hooked.

All can be achieved by blocking the attacker's vision.

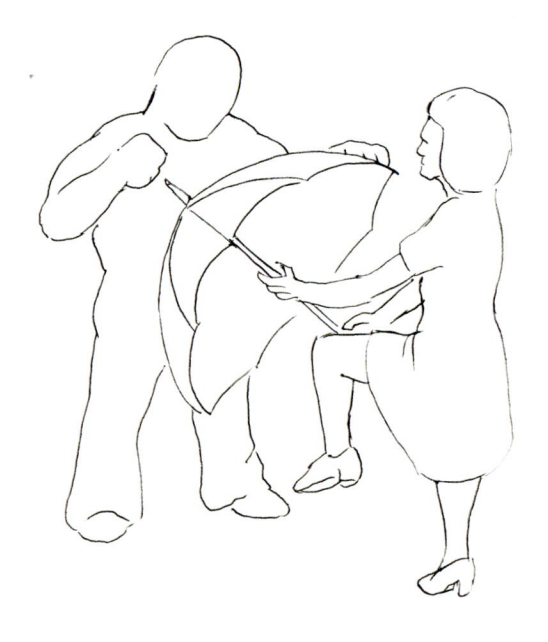

Left is shown an ineffective defence with the umbrella which is soft and bends easily.

The correct techniques for an effective defence are shown below.

For both techniques, put your whole bodyweight into the movement.

High heel shoe

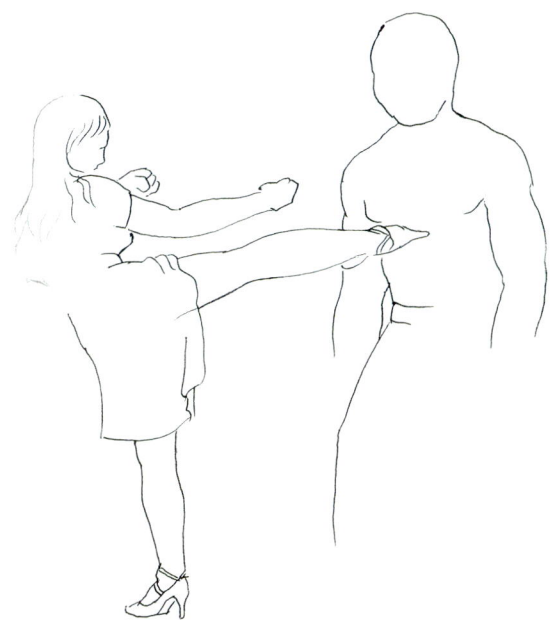

Sidekick

Scarf string rope

Chair

Here is shown the right and wrong ways to defend oneself with a chair.

Use the legs of the chair to penetrate, and put your bodyweight into the movement, pictured left.

Not like this >>

Striking an assailant with a chair.

As shown on the left, lead with the seat of the chair. This is much harder to block.

Not like this >>

CHAPTER VI:
SPECIAL SKILLS

Belt

As 'ball and chain'.

This flexible weapon can reach around an attacker's guard easily to cause shock.

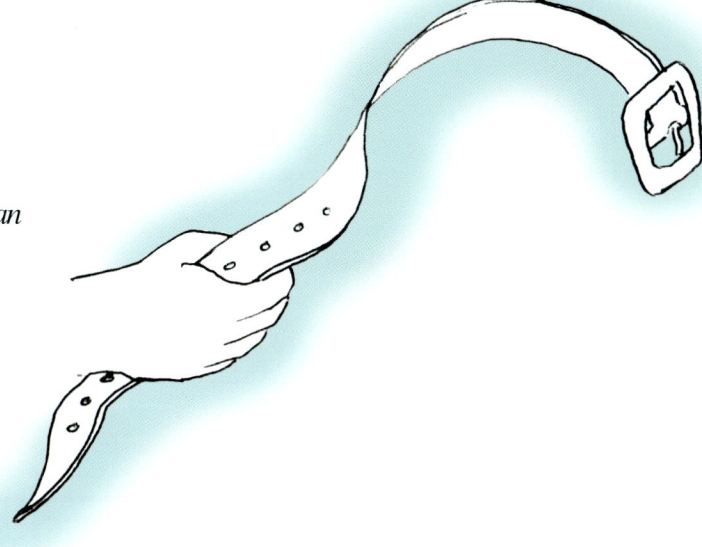

Keys

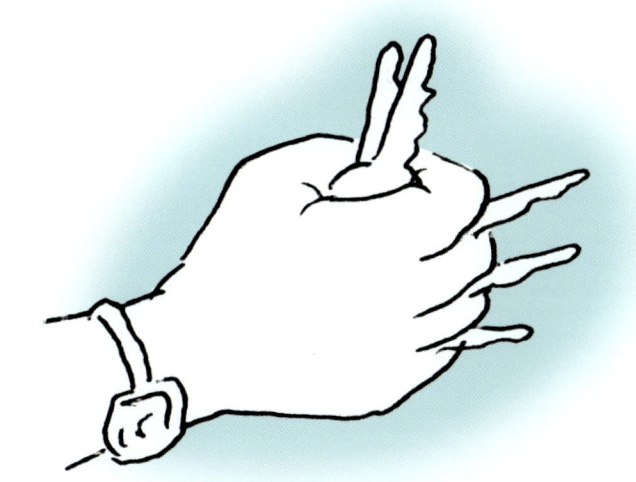

This weapon can cause extreme pain. Use it suddenly and without warning for best effects.

121

CHAPTER VI:
SPECIAL SKILLS

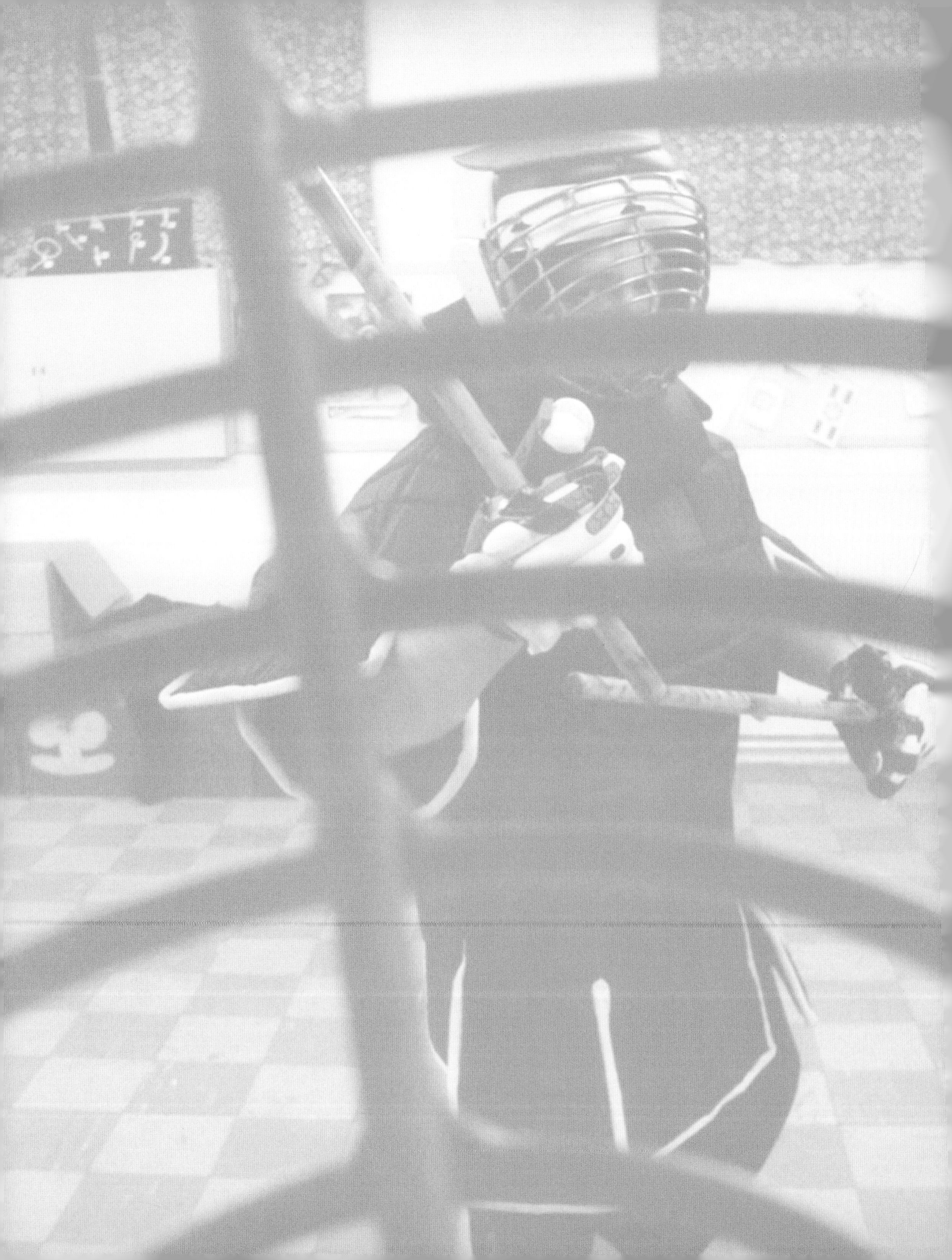

CHAPTER VII: THE SYLLABUS

In this chapter we see what is required to enable a fighter to be distinguished as an English Combat exponent from the level of beginner to one that would make them an adept or instructor. It is recommended that the fighter travel to England to attend training with Terry Glover on occasion. If this is not possible then a DVD can be purchased to accompany the book. Please look on the following website www.englishcombat.com.

Instructor Assessment

The fighter must supply the critical observer with the following.

Submit a current First Aid certificate from a Health and Safety Course (England).

Submit a current in date English Combat Licence that shows the following:

- All other grades have been successfully completed and recorded.

- An entry, that the applicant took part, as a fighter, in either a semi, or full contact weapons or unarmed competition.

Complete a written question paper with time allowed of one hour and achieve a score of 80% or more to ascertain underpinning subject knowledge (this would need to be fifty questions from all aspects of the system).

Given a training hall scenario, the student is to correct the area according to Health and Safety requirements (England).

The applicant is to explain to the assessor how to check a student licence. This would mean checking the ability ascertained to date and that insurance is correct, adequate and paid to date. That the licence belongs to the fighter and contains an appropriate photograph to identify the fighter.

The applicant will give a twenty-minute lesson, to include both unarmed and armed instruction. Technique and weapon taught to be chosen by applicant.

Perform a defence against a group of armed and unarmed attackers. Applicant to begin unarmed.

Syllabus - Part One

Basics

Unarmed – With a partner – Both sides of the body

        Attack   *Counter*

1. Step in, punch to the head – Step back, upper block, cross punch to the body.
2. Step in, punch to the body – Step back, inner block, back fist to the temple.
3. Step in, punch to the body – Step back, outer block, cross punch to the body.
4. Step in, punch to the body – Step back, inner down block, cross punch to the ribs.
5. Snap punch to the head – Slide in, brush block, cross punch to the ribs.
6. Quick dart, cross punch to the body – Dart in oblique, back fist to the head.
7. Front kick to the body – Slide back inner downward block, ridge hand to the face.
8. Roundhouse kick to the body – Dart in oblique, cross punch to the body.
9. Side-kick to the body – Slide back double press block.

Armed – With a partner – Both sides of the body

1. Quarterstaff, 1-12   - Block with Long Staff using thirds, hands still.
2. Short Staff, 1-12   - Block by jamming.
3. Knife, 1-12   - Block with knife and live hand.

Combinations

Unarmed – With a partner – Both sides of the body

1. Snap punch to the head, step up front kick (front leg) to the body.
2. Step up front kick (front leg) reverse punch to the body.

Armed – Short Staff – With a partner – Both sides of the body

1. No 1 double arc, No 4 snap hit and double circle (show footwork).
2. Strike No 1, 2 - thrust No 5 - fan to the head - strike No 8 - thrust No 9.

Syllabus - Part Two

Basics

Unarmed – With a partner – Both sides of the body

1. Step in, punch to the head – Step back, upper block, cross punch to the ribs, wrist lock take down, immobilise neck.
2. Step in, punch to the body – Step back, inner block, back fist to the head, (Hold with free hand) wrist lock take down.
3. Step in punch to the body – Step back outer block, hook, cross punch, step through, elbow strike and roll, wrist lock take down, immobilize neck.
4. Step in, punch to the body – Step back, inner down block, cross punch to ribs, wrist lock take down.
5. Snap punch to the head – Slide in, brush block, reverse punch to the armpit, double hand head grab, two alternate knee kicks to the face.
6. Dart in, cross punch to body – Front hand down block, back hand back fist to temple.
7. Front kick to the body – Slide back inner down block, ridge hand to the face, tug down shoulder and back hand sweep away leg to take down, keep hold and edge of hand to the face followed by two punches as a triple strike.
8. Roundhouse kick to the body – Catch, step through, put down, stomp on groin, throw away the leg.
9. Side kick to the body – Slide in, scoop leg, sweep supporting leg and dump the body followed down to punch face and hammer punch groin.

Armed – With a partner – Both sides of the body

1. Quarter Staff – Long range 1 – 12 – Block long range, then numbers and block and counter for one minute (B & C).
2. Short Staff – Range drill to butt strike, then No's and B & C for one minute.
3. Knife – 1 – 12 strip, then No's and B & C for one minute.

Combinations

Unarmed – With a partner – Both sides of the body

1. Step up, front leg roundhouse, back leg side kick, back fist to the head.
2. Dart in, punch head body, step up front kick.

Armed

Quarter Staff – 1. Demonstrate rotation drill around the body, both arms.
– 2. Long range attack B & C.

Short Staff – Rap 4-2, strike 7. Rap 3-1 Strike 8 (Reverse for left hand)

Knife – 1. Blade up, 1 min cut and thrust.
– 2. Blade down, 1 min cut & thrust.

Light Sparring – 1 – 2 minutes

Syllabus - Part Three

Basics

Unarmed

1. Demonstrate release from grabs and holds to arms body and throat. (Student's choice)
2. Demonstrate and explain attacks to various parts of the body using the correct technique for the correct target. (Students choice)
3. Demonstrate – Arm bar, Head lock, Wrist lock, Leg lock, Arrest hold.
4. Demonstrate – Shoulder strike, Buttocks strike.
5. Explain with demonstrations how body weight is put into punches and kicks. (Students to choose three punches and three kicks to be submitted prior to the exam)

Armed - All weapon sequences to last for three rounds of one minute with thirty seconds rest in between each.

1. Quarter Staff – Demonstrate slow attacks to partner at long, medium and short range – partner demonstrates defence techniques.
2. Short staff – Demonstrate slow attacks to partner at long, medium and short range – partner demonstrates defence techniques.
3. Knife – Demonstrate slow attacks to partner at all ranges, they show defence.

Combinations

Unarmed – (Full speed)

1. One minute showing attack with selected techniques on a hanging bag to demonstrate application of power.

Armed – (Full speed) – Thirty seconds rest between rounds.

1. Quarter Staff – One minute showing full contact on hanging bag to demonstrate application of power.
2. Short staff – One minute showing full contact on hanging bag to demonstrate application of power, speed and variety of technique.
3. Knife – Demonstrate ability to throw knife by blade and hilt, through one revolution at target card. Knife to penetrate a minimum of two out of three permitted throws.

Syllabus - Part Four

Weapon Demonstration

1. Show ability to crack whip three times in succession with each arm.
2. Show ability to grab stick with the whip and disarm. (Partner to remain still)
3. Show the ability to trip standing person with whip.
4. Show how the whip can be used for close quarter blocking and attack.
5. Show 1 – 12 flail (Single ball)
6. Show blocking of attacks 1 – 12 with the flail (Single ball)
7. Demonstrate the ability to embed an axe two out of three throws at a nominated target and strike two out of three throws. (Minimum of six and one half paces)
8. Demonstrate an ability to throw a Quarterstaff at a nominated target and strike two out of three throws. (Minimum of six and one half paces)
9. Demonstrate an ability to throw a knife and embed by the hilt and by the blade two out of three throws.

Disarms

1. Quarter staff – Demonstrate disarms 1 – 12

    a) Medium range
    b) Butt range

Free Fighting

1. Fighting semi contact, unarmed with a partner for two rounds with thirty seconds break between rounds. (No grappling or holding)
2. Fighting slow, with a Quarter Staff, with a partner, for two rounds with thirty seconds between rounds.
3. Fighting slow, with a Short staff, with a partner, two rounds with thirty seconds between rounds.
4. Fighting slow with knives with a partner for two rounds with thirty seconds between rounds.

COMPETITION CRITERIA

When practicing together it is advisable to hold a competition for good feedback. This way you can fight full contact within boundaries that ensure safe conduct.

To hold a competition there must be one referee and three judges.

The competition area shall be not less than that comprising one half of a Badminton court.

The fighters must be properly armored when using weapons.

The Armour comprising of, Helmet, Body Armour, Groin Box, Elbow Pads, well padded Gloves and Forearm Protection must be well maintained and in good order.

When not using weapons but not grappling, the same area is used with protection the same except for the Helmet and Body Armour.

When not using weapons and including grappling then no protection is used at all. The area would however be covered in suitable matting unless it was to be held outdoors and then common sense will prevail to find suitable soft ground.

The Judges will determine the scoring. The points awarded for each round will be 10.

The points will be awarded as 10 to the winner of each round and 9 to the loser.

In the event of a draw then one more round is fought and only one winner declared by the judges.

Disarming an opponent will cause one point to be removed from the disarmed fighters card. Two disarms will constitute a win for the fighter who carries them out.

Three warnings for illegal techniques will constitute a loss.

Target area for weapons will be from the top of the head to the bottom of the armour.

Target area for unarmed fights will be the front of head only and no neck. Then the area of the body down to the waistband is also a target. Foot-sweeps are allowed on agreement between the fighters concerned. Use of thrusting and butt is also upon common agreement. Grappling will continue until one fighter taps out or capitulates.

FULL CONTACT WEAPON FIGHTING: THE RULES

1. Each fighter must know the rules without exception.

2. Each fighter must be correctly insured and in date. The insurance must be checked prior to the preliminary bouts.

3. Each fighter must possess and wear proper Armour for protection.

4. Each fighter must give quarter to the opponent who is fairly beaten.

5. Each fighter failing to show courtesy and good manners will be named a loser on completion of a bout.

6. Each fighter that loses his or her temper will be disqualified.

7. Each fighter will only strike from the top of the head to the knee including the arms and hands.

8. Each fighter will avoid striking to the back of the head and body.

9. Each fighter will observe gallantry and not strike an opponent who has the back of the head or body exposed accidentally.

10. Each fighter taking advantage of the opposing fighter's gallantry by recklessly exposing the back to obtain dastardly advantage shall be disqualified and listed in the training hall as a coward and duly shamed.

11. Each fighter that is disarmed within two seconds shall lose one point within that round.

12. Each fighter being disarmed twice shall lose the bout.

13. Bouts will last for three rounds of one-minute duration, with thirty seconds break in between each round.

14. Each fighter will not unfairly hold onto the opponent.

15. Each fighter can use the live hand to affect a check strike but make sure it does not constitute a push. The referee shall decide which is which.

16. The bout will have one referee who shall ensure the rules are complied with and look after the safety of the fighters.

17. The bout shall have three judges who will mark a scorecard.

18. Cards will hold a tally of ten points for each fighter and in the event of a draw shall need to judge a further one round.

19. During an extra round in the case of a draw, the judges must choose one fighter as the winner.

20. In the event of a complaint or indecision the referee shall decide the winner, no argument.

21. Each fighter will be scored between seven to ten points per round.

22. The point score is awarded for the following;

   i. Landing a clean single unopposed strike to the target area.

   ii. Landing a clean unopposed striking combination.

   iii. Blocking a strike and making a counter strike.

   iv. Showing good nimble footwork helping successful strikes.

   v. Showing dexterity with a variety of striking combinations.

   vi. Using the live hand to effectively check an opponent's arms and body to control the opponent and affect a win.

   vii. Effectively and quickly disarm the opponent's weapon within two seconds of the attempt.

A timekeeper will indicate the end of each round by bell/whistle, and will time the bout.

THE COMPETITION AREA

The competition area shall comprise of an area not more than twenty-five yards long and twenty-five yards wide.

The opponents will start the bout with weapons touching in the centre of the fighting area and the referee holding the weapons together.

On the command, 'Fight', the bout will commence.

On the command, 'Stop', the bout will stop.

On the command, 'Break', the opponents will separate.

Failure to obey the referee shall incur a warning.

Failure to obey the warning shall incur a penalty point.

Failure to obey the referee consistently shall incur disqualification.

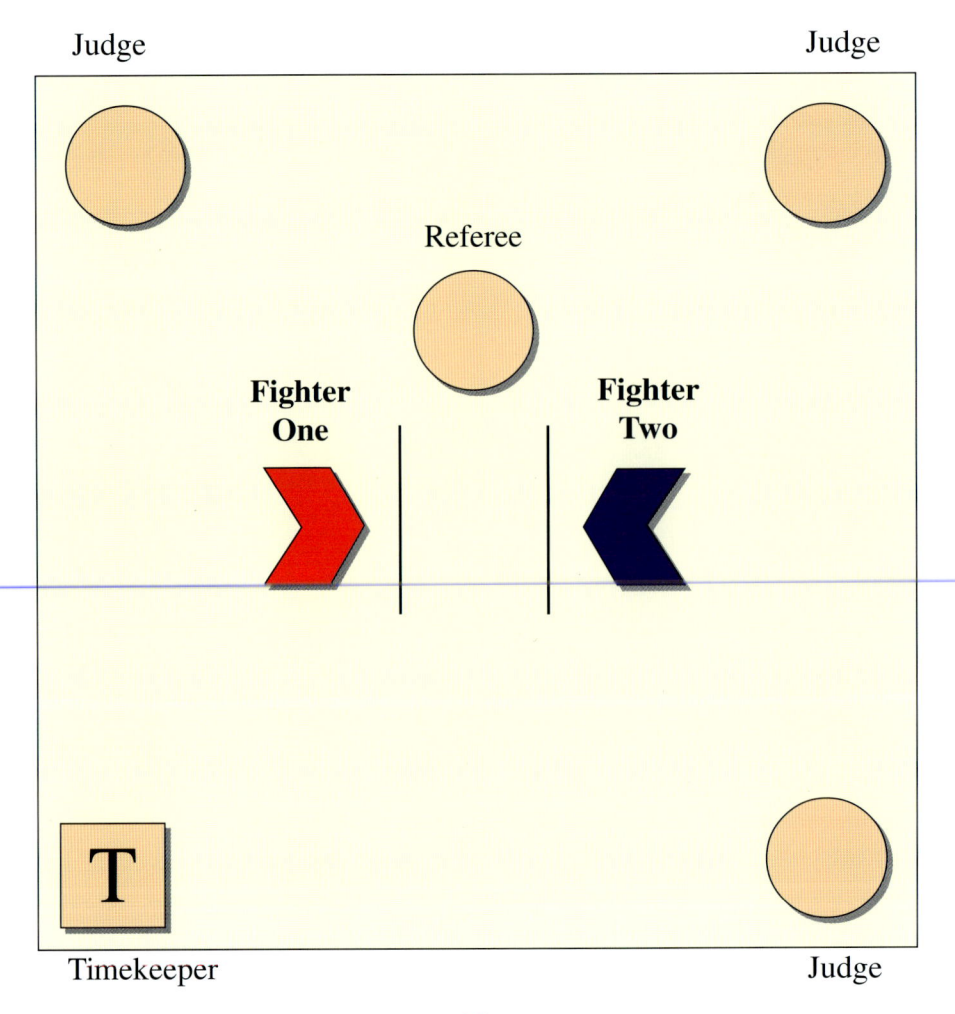

English Combat Order Form

If you would like to order **hard copy editions** of the syllabus, or any other item from English Combat, just fill in the details below and send this form to the address shown at the end. Alternatively, you can order electronic and hard copy editions of books, and all other items online at www.englishcombat.com.

Item	Price	Qty	Sub-Total
The English Combat Training Book ISBN 0-9547404-3-2 **By Terry Glover B.E.M.** *Fully illustrated, 130 pages* The English Fighting System for self defence and competition, English Combat teaches use of the English Quarterstaff, Single Stick, Double Stick, Knife, Axe, Whip, Ball and Chain and unarmed combat. The empty hand element utilises kicks, strikes, blocks, sweeps, throws, locks, elbow and knee strikes. Bringing together English fighting techniques from all ages that made the Englishman the World's most feared and respected fighter. [EC002]	£19.99 each		
Scouts Master at Arms Activity Badge: Syllabus for English Quarterstaff and Single Stick ISBN 0-9547404-1-6 **By Terry Glover B.E.M.** *Fully illustrated, 40 pages* The skills, techniques and training necessary for attainment of the Scout Master at Arms Activity Badge in the use of English Quarterstaff and Single Stick, as originally advocated by Robert Baden-Powell. [EC001]	£9.99 each		
English Combat: T-shirt English Combat logo and web address on left chest pocket area; full-size logo on reverse. Black only. State size: S, M, L, XL [ECTS1]	£12.99 each		
English Combat: Mouse Mat English Combat logo on black background. [ECMM1]	£5.99 each		

(All prices shown in GBP and correct at time of publication)

* Grand Total: £ ☐

* Plus postage and packing (see below)

Delivery, Postage and Packing Charges: Wherever you are in the world your goods should usually be received within 14 days, but please allow up to 28 days. For the UK, Royal Mail or Parcel Post is suitable and is quick and inexpensive. International Parcel Post is our service for the rest of the world, sent at standard minimum rates.

Returns Policy: Claims for apparent defects must be notified within 3 days of receipt by the Buyer of the goods and will only be accepted by the Seller if the goods are still in their original state and have not been treated or processed. Claims for latent defects must be notified within 3 days of receipt of goods or immediately after identification whichever be the earlier.

I choose to make payment by (please tick):

Credit/Debit Card ____   Cheque/Postal Order ____   International Money Order ____

- Cheques payable to "**English Combat**"
- Your credit card details will be securely disposed of by English Combat when your order is completed.

Continue overleaf...

Billing Address:	**Delivery Address** (if different)**:**
Name:	Name: ....
Delivery Address:	Delivery Address: ....
....	....
....	....
Country:	Country: ....
Post/Zip Code:	Post/Zip Code: ....
Contact Email:	

Credit/Debit Card Details:

Please tick: ❑ Mastercard   ❑ Visa   ❑ Delta   ❑ Electron   ❑ JCB   ❑ Solo   ❑ Switch

Card Number: ☐☐☐☐ ☐☐☐☐ ☐☐☐☐ ☐☐☐☐

Valid From: ☐☐ / ☐☐   Issue Number (Solo/Switch): ☐☐

Expiry Date: ☐☐ / ☐☐   Security Code: ☐☐

Signed: ....   Date: ....

Please check that all details are correct, and send your completed order form to:

English Combat
24 Hoe View Road
Nottingham
NG12 3DF
UK

(REF: TRAINING BOOK)

❑ Tick here if you do not wish to receive promotional correspondence from English Combat or other selected businesses.
We may have to share some of your personal information if one of the following conditions applies:
1. Delivery of your items requires that we share some information, such as address, with a shipper.
2. We are legally required to release information, as by the order of a court or another governmental authoritative requirement.